A LOCAL'S G

BLOODLINE

BRAD BERTELLI

DAVID SLOAN

PHANTOM PRESS
KEYWEST

For use of information contained as source material, credit: David L. Sloan and Brad Bertelli, authors, *A Local's Guide To Bloodline.*

Editorial services: DorothyDrennen.com

Inquiries: david@phantompress.com

ISBN: 978-0-9831671-5-0

HOW TO USE

1. **WHAT TO EXPECT**

   This guide is comprehensive and includes the majority of Bloodline film locations in the Florida Keys from Season 1 and Season 2. Some of the locations are fantastic stops featured multiple times and easily recognizable. Others appeared briefly and are unremarkable apart from their Bloodline affiliation. Don't hesitate to pick and choose from your favorite scenes.

2. **MILE MARKERS**

   Most directions in the Florida Keys involve Mile Markers. Mile Marker 0 is in Key West. Mile Marker 108 is in Key Largo. To get a sense of what Mile Marker a location is near, remove the last three digits from its listed address.

3. **OCEANSIDE AND BAYSIDE**

   Local directions will often include *Oceanside* or *Bayside*. When you drive south along the Overseas Highway, Bayside, or Florida Bay, is on your right. As you drive north, Oceanside, or the Atlantic Ocean, is on your right.

4. **FIRST FEATURED**

   The *First Featured* section for each location tells you when and where the location appeared so you can watch the scene on your phone or tablet.

5. **KNOW BEFORE YOU GO**

   While most locations are accessible and open to the public, some are private or just do not have time to deal with sightseers. Check the *Getting There* section for each location before you go so you know what to expect.

6. **SPOILER ALERT**

   This book contains plot details from Seasons 1 and 2.

LOCATION LIST

1. THE OVERSEAS HIGHWAY
2. PARK MOTEL
3. ALABAMA JACK'S SIDE SHACK
4. ALABAMA JACK'S
5. JEWFISH CREEK BRIDGE
6. O'BANNON'S HOUSE
7. CARIBBEAN CLUB
8. PENNEKAMP PARK (CHRIST OF THE DEEP)
9. CORAL FINANCIAL JEWELRY AND PAWN
10. DENNY'S LATIN CAFE
11. MRS. MAC'S KITCHEN II
12. STONE LEDGE PARADISE INN
13. VAUGHN BUILDING
14. SUNRISE CUBAN CAFE
15. CAFE MOKA
16. MARINER'S HOSPITAL
17. PLANTATION KEY COURTHOUSE
18. ISLAND HOME NURSERY
19. MARLIN FOOD STORES
20. TOM THUMB
21. MARKER 88
22. POSTNET
23. FOUNDERS PARK
24. SEASON 3 HIDEOUT
25. HOG HEAVEN

LOCATION LIST

MAP

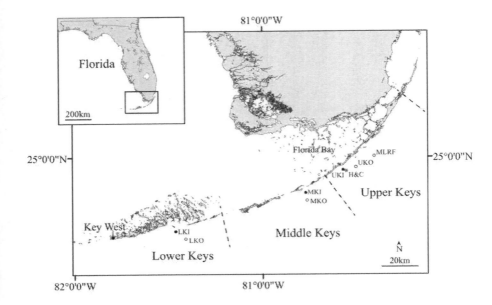

Most film locations are in the Upper Keys section of the above map. This section includes Islamorada and Key Largo. Locations in this guide are listed geographically from north to south, with number 1 being the northernmost location. Mile Markers for each city are listed below.

KEY LARGO: 108-91
ISLAMORADA: 90-66
MARATHON: 65-40
BIG PINE KEY: 39-9
KEY WEST: 8-0

THE WATER
LETS YOU IN

BLOODLINE THEME BY BOOK OF FEARS

YOUNG MAN GOES OUT LOOKING
FOR THE DIAMOND IN THE SEA.
OLD MAN ROWS HIS BOAT TO SHORE
AND FALLS ON TWISTED KNEES.

AND YOU'LL DROWN BEFORE
THE WATER LETS YOU IN...
YOU'LL DROWN BEFORE
THE WATER LETS YOU IN...

THE FEELING THAT I FEAR THE MOST
IS THE ONE THAT FOLLOWS ME.
ALL ACROSS THE STARRY COAST
FROM SEA TO DYING SEA. IT SAYS...

YOU'LL DROWN BEFORE
THE WATER LETS YOU IN...
YOU'LL DROWN BEFORE
THE WATER LETS YOU IN...

I THINK THE THING I'VE WANTED MOST
WAS JUST NEVER MEANT TO BE.
A THOUSAND WAVES, A THOUSAND GHOSTS
THEIR SORROWS FOLLOW ME.

AND YOU'LL DROWN BEFORE
THE WATER LETS YOU IN...
YOU'LL DROWN BEFORE
THE WATER LETS YOU IN...

1

THE OVERSEAS HIGHWAY
KEY LARGO TO KEY WEST

THE SCENE

In 2009, the Overseas Highway was declared one of just 30 "All-American Roads" by the Federal Highway Administration. It is only fitting that one of North America's most scenic drives plays a pivotal role in a series embracing the Florida Keys.

BEHIND THE SCENE

The highway first opened to traffic between the mainland and Key West in 1928. In those days the trip required a long drive followed by a 40-mile ferry ride between Lower Matecumbe and No Name keys. After the horrific 1935 Labor Day Hurricane, the highway was redesigned with a solid bridge system that made the ferry obsolete. The highway reopened in 1938.

GETTING THERE

The only way to drive up and down the Keys is on the Overseas Highway. Exit the Florida Turnpike at its southernmost terminus and drive straight. Take it slow and see why this is one of the most beautiful drives in the country.

FIRST FEATURED

Multiple aerial and ground scenes throughout series.

WILD MARKERS?

Locals watching the first episodes of Bloodline quickly realized that Mile Markers shown in the episodes did not accurately reflect the featured locations.

2

PARK MOTEL
600 S. KROME AVENUE
HOMESTEAD
(305) 247-6731

THE SCENE

One of several hotels featured in the show. Kevin uses the Park Motel as a hideout after Lowry discovers he has been selling his stolen cocaine. Meg shows up to help him, and Kevin manages to escape.

BEHIND THE SCENE

While much of Bloodline is filmed in the Keys, this hotel is found on the mainland in Homestead. The area includes several budget motels, but the Park Motel is a classic. For those hard core fans looking to see every Bloodline locale, save this one for the beginning of the drive to the keys, or the drive out of the Keys.

GETTING THERE

Homestead is located on the mainland near the terminus of the turnpike. This is the northernmost locale featured in this guide. The hotel is located on the corner of Krome Avenue and 6th Street. GPS is your friend on this one.

FIRST FEATURED

Part 16 | 19:11

WATCH OUT

Norbert Leo Butz *(Kevin Rayburn)* did not initially watch Bloodline and remained mostly unaware of the story arcs that didn't involve his character. Last minute script changes were common.

3

THE BUS STOP
58000 CARD SOUND ROAD
NORTH KEY LARGO

THE SCENE

Danny Rayburn is sitting on a bus bound for the Keys when it makes a stop. Outside the bus a sign advertises bus tickets, fishing licenses, tourist information, and live bait. Danny asks the old timer out front how much it would cost for a ticket back to Miami. After paying the $27.50, he steps back outside and sees his parents' photograph on the front page of the *Island Gazette*.

BEHIND THE SCENE

Set designers worked their magic to transform this concrete structure into the bus stop.

GETTING THERE

The 18-Mile Stretch, following the original line of Henry Flagler's railroad, is the quicker route to Key Largo. The Card Sound Road is more scenic, but includes a $1 toll. Card Sound follows the original route of the Overseas Highway and will deliver you to Alabama Jack's. Though the interior of the bus station building, located in the parking lot of Alabama Jack's, is not accessible, the bar is. Step in for some of their world famous conch fritters.

FIRST FEATURED

Part 1 | 7:48

SISSY SIGHTING

Sissy Spaceck *(Sally Rayburn)* stayed just off of Card Sound Road in a vacation rental at North Key Largo's Ocean Reef Club during Bloodline filming.

4

ALABAMA JACK'S
58000 CARD SOUND ROAD
KEY LARGO
ALABAMAJACKS.COM | (305) 248-8741

THE SCENE

While his brother is waiting for him further down the Keys, Danny disembarks from the bus at a North Key Largo bus stop. After contemplating returning to Miami, he goes to Alabama Jack's and sits at the bar for a bite and a cold drink. While sipping his beer, Danny complains to the waitress about his not-so-fresh grouper taco. This is also the location where Eric O'Bannon, Danny's best friend, first shows up.

BEHIND THE SCENE

Jack Stratham was a riveter who helped build the Empire State Building. Because of his southern drawl, he earned the nickname "Alabama Jack." After settling in what was once the Card Sound community, Jack opened his bar and restaurant in the 1950s. Step inside for some authentic Conch atmosphere.

GETTING THERE

When entering the Keys from the Card Sound Road route, drive until you see the tollbooth. Alabama Jack's is a classic dive bar, but closes around sunset when the mosquitoes start biting.

FIRST FEATURED

Part 1 | 9:30

IN THE ZONE

Portions of the main bar at Alabama Jack's were originally built as part of a set for the 1994 Wesley Snipes action film *Drop Zone.*

5

JEWFISH
CREEK BRIDGE
107800 OVERSEAS HIGHWAY
KEY LARGO

THE SCENE

A beer-drinking fisherman looks down from his spot on the bridge and sees a body floating in the water. When the Monroe County Sheriff arrives to investigate, we learn that this is the second badly burned Hispanic body found in the water. In another scene under the bridge, Rafi confesses to Danny that he burned the boat filled with immigrants.

BEHIND THE SCENE

The first Jewfish Creek Bridge was built for the Over-Sea Railway circa 1907. The bridge has undergone several incarnations; the current bridge opened in 2008, more than 100 years after the original. The Jersey barriers separating traffic of those entering the Keys from those leaving were painted Belize Blue, a color selected by artist Robert Wyland. Wyland is famous for his Whaling Walls, one of which can be seen at Mile Marker 99 in the median of the Overseas Highway.

GETTING THERE

To find the fishing spot, take the Yacht Club Drive exit off of the Jewfish Creek Bridge at Mile Marker 107.8. Several scenes were filmed here beneath the overpass.

FIRST FEATURED

Part 4 | 35:02

UNDER THE INFLUENCE

The creators of *Bloodline* cite *Crime and Punishment* as a major narrative influence on their show.

6

CASA O'BANNON
7 PARADISE ROAD
KEY LARGO
PRIVATE RESIDENCE

THE SCENE

This location served as the home of Eric O'Bannon and his sister Chelsea O'Bannon. It is featured in dozens of scenes, including visits from all of the Rayburn brothers on different occasions.

BEHIND THE SCENE

This home is a private residence.

GETTING THERE

Paradise Drive is found near Mile Marker 105, Bayside. The house is the last one on the right, situated on a corner property with the main house on Coral Way. This is a private residence. Do not trespass. Respect the residents.

FIRST FEATURED

Part 2, 11:49

PARTY TIME

While filming Season 1, the cast and crew of Bloodline held their holiday party at The OceanView Pub. The OceanView was a favorite filming location.

7

THE CARIBBEAN CLUB
104080 OVERSEAS HIGHWAY
KEY LARGO
CARIBBEANCLUBKL.COM | (305) 451-4466

THE SCENE
The World Famous Caribbean Club appears in Parts 3, 5, and 8. Danny and Chelsea, his best friend's sister, play pool and flirt here. Meg reveals to Kevin that Marco already knows about his relationship troubles, though Kevin does not seem to care. He is just happy to be free. Danny meets Rafi here in Part 8.

BEHIND THE SCENE
The Caribbean Club opened as a fishing lodge in 1940. While no scenes from the movie *Key Largo* were ever filmed on site, the script was written here. Jimmy Buffett is famously said to have said, "It was a bar like many others and then it wasn't."

GETTING THERE
Arrive by bike, car or boat. The Caribbean Club is located close to Mile Marker 104, Bayside. They serve from morning until night (7AM to 4AM most days). The bar is cash only but there is an ATM on site.

FIRST FEATURED
Part 3 | 44:28

ACT YOUR AGE
Ben Mendelsohn plays the oldest of the Rayburn brothers, but is in fact the youngest of the actors. Ben was born in 1969, Kyle Chandler in 1965, and Norbert Leo Butz in 1967.

8

PENNEKAMP PARK
(CHRIST OF THE DEEP)
102601 OVERSEAS HIGHWAY
KEY LARGO

FLORIDASTATEPARKS.ORG/PARK/PENNEKAMP.COM

(305) 451-6300

THE SCENE

Danny Rayburn takes guests of the Rayburn House on a snorkeling adventure. When they jump overboard with their masks and snorkels, they swim past the most photographed underwater image in the Florida Keys, the Christ of the Deep. The statue, placed within the John Pennekamp Coral Reef State Park in 1965, sits in 25 feet of water in the area known as Key Largo Dry Rocks.

BEHIND THE SCENE

Established in 1963, Pennekamp was the first undersea park in the United States. It is within the Florida Keys National Marine Sanctuary. The statue is some 20 miles north of the Rayburn House.

GETTING THERE

The park is open daily from 8AM until sunset. Admission is $8 per vehicle. Look for the park entrance at Mile Marker 102.5, Oceanside. Don't let the adult toy store across the street distract you. Snorkeling and boat trips are available from the park. Call in advance to reserve your spot on the boat. Make sure the statue is on the charter's itinerary for that day!

FIRST FEATURED

Part 3 | 35:59

DON'T FORGET THE KEYS

On choosing the Florida Keys as the film location, co-creator Todd A. Kessler said, "We were looking for a place to set the show that had kind of an iconic sensibility for the United States, if not the world."

9

CORAL FINANCIAL
JEWELRY & PAWN
102071 OVERSEAS HIGHWAY
KEY LARGO
(305) 453-5300

THE SCENE
A scene with the famous seahorse charm necklace was filmed here. Eric comes in to pawn a Hummel figurine he stole from his mother in hopes of retrieving the seahorse charm necklace he pawned before he left town.

BEHIND THE SCENE
This is a pretty cool pawnshop and is usually stocked with a good selection of bicycles, guitars, and items you might only find in the Keys.

GETTING THERE
Located at Mile Marker 102, Oceanside, look for the yellow awning with black letters advertising pawn. They are open 9AM to 6PM most days but they are closed on Sundays. The shop opens at noon on Tuesdays.

FIRST FEATURED
Part 22 | 24:32

UNDERLYING THEME
The moody Bloodline opening song is *The Water Let's You In* by Book of Fears. The band was named after a book written by a paranoid schizophrenic who once lived in a home for the mentally disabled.

10

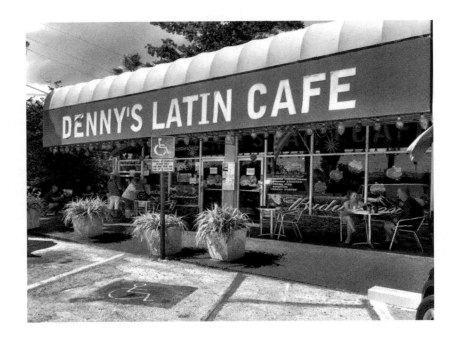

DENNY'S LATIN CAFE
99600 OVERSEAS HIGHWAY
KEY LARGO
(305) 451-3665

THE SCENE
Ralph Lawler is seated at a table at Denny's when he calls Danny on an untraceable burner phone. He gives Danny instructions for what to do with Lowry's drugs.

BEHIND THE SCENE
Denny's Latin Café should not be confused with Denny's just down the road. Denny's Latin Cafe serves up great Latin food with a menu full of favorites. Try the Cuban coffee and the Cuban sandwich, but make sure you save room for flan.

GETTING THERE
Watch for the red and yellow awnings at Mile Marker 99.6, Bayside. Denny's Latin Cafe is open from 6AM to 10PM every day.

FIRST FEATURED
Part 11 | 16:45

CASTING CALL OF DUTY
Tyler Cravens *(Ralph Lawler)* continued his career, which included performing as a stand up comedian, after returning as a combat veteran from the Gulf War.

MRS. MAC'S
KITCHEN II
99020 OVERSEAS HIGHWAY
KEY LARGO
MRSMACSKITCHEN.COM | (305) 451-6227

THE SCENE
When Danny and Chelsea meet here for breakfast, he offers her money to help cover the rent at her mother's house. Accustomed to Danny's ways, Chelsea refuses the offer, telling him she can't be with him if he is headed for trouble. Jane Rayburn and Evangeline Radosevich also meet here in Season 2 when Evangeline gives Jane the shirt she stole from a consignment shop.

BEHIND THE SCENE
The original Mrs. Mac's can be found across the street. Popularity led to expansion. They have been serving up great local grub since 1976 and boast 25 wines by the glass and a full bar.

GETTING THERE
Mrs. Mac's II can be found in the median of the Overseas Highway at Mile Marker 99. Look for the salmon colored building with a sign across the top that says, "Eat well, laugh often, live long." Open Monday through Saturday from 11AM to 10PM. Closed Sunday.

FIRST FEATURED
Part 10 | 33:34

STAR WARS
Andrea Riseborough *(Evangeline Radosevich)* describes her character as "She's like the Death Star that sucks you in in 'Star Wars.' "

12

STONE LEDGE
PARADISE INN
95320 OVERSEAS HIGHWAY
KEY LARGO
STONELEDGEPARADISEINN.COM | (305) 852-8114

THE SCENE

For Bloodline, this mom and pop motel was named the Red Reef Motel and is featured in several episodes. Both Eric O'Bannon and Danny Rayburn hide out here while Lowry's men search for Danny. Ralph Lawler, hired by Lowry to kill Danny, finds him at the hotel. Danny turns the tables on Lawler and kills him with a conch shell. John Rayburn watches Danny's room from the inn's parking lot.

BEHIND THE SCENE

The inn's real name is the Stone Ledge Paradise Inn. It is one of the few remaining 1950's style resorts in the area. Located on Florida Bay, the motel offers 21 rooms, picnic areas, a dock, and a boat ramp. Bloodline filmed room 21 at the rear of the property.

GETTING THERE

The sign with a sunset background and a heart hanging from it is set back from the highway at Mile Marker 95.3, Bayside. A stone marker with a painted marlin also marks the entrance here.

FIRST FEATURED

Part 12 | 27:56

BLIND AUDITION

Ralph Lawler is played by actor Tyler Cravens. Originally, the role had no name and was described as "white haired man." Tyler Cravens had little to go on in his audition, as the creators looked to keep plot details a secret.

13

VAUGHN BUILDING
92410 OVERSEAS HIGHWAY
TAVERNIER

THE SCENE
During his campaign for sheriff, John Rayburn's election headquarters is located on the second floor of this strip plaza. At this location John first encounters Ozzy Delveccio posing as a lost tourist. Ozzy later returns to the office to extort Meg.

BEHIND THE SCENE
The Vaughn Building is a 12-unit plaza with a variety of businesses.

GETTING THERE
The building sits somewhat perpendicular to the Overseas Highway and does not feature any prominent signs to identify it. Driving south, the building can be spotted near Mile Marker 92.4, Bayside. If you drive past Chad's Deli, you have driven too far.

FIRST FEATURED
Part 18 | 35:35

ALL THE BUZZ
"I don't mind the heat as long as the mosquitoes aren't out."
— Linda Cardellini *(Meg Rayburn)* on summer in the Florida Keys

SUNRISE CUBAN CAFE
91885 OVERSEAS HIGHWAY
TAVERNIER
SUNRISECUBANCAFE.COM | (305) 852-7216

THE SCENE

Meg meets a former Rayburn employee, Carlos, who tries to convince her to represent him. Carlos has been charged with larceny and aggravated assault. He blames his problems on drinking but assures Meg that he has quit. Meg reluctantly accepts his case.

BEHIND THE SCENE

The Sunrise Market serves up some of the best authentic Cuban food in the Keys with time-tested and authentic recipes. Don't leave without trying the Cuban coffee that locals call *con leche*.

GETTING THERE

Located next to the Old Settlers Park, Sunrise is open from 5AM to 9PM, seven days a week. Turn off of the Overseas Highway at Mile Marker 91.8, Oceanside, and watch for the bank of newspaper machines and a sandwich board sign advertising Cuban coffee.

FIRST FEATURED

Part 6 | 19:41

FEEL THE BURN

A Miami native, Eliezer Castro had walk-on roles in *Burn Notice* and *Graceland* before landing the role of Carlos Mejia.

15

CAFE MOKA
91865 OVERSEAS HIGHWAY
TAVERNIER
(305) 453-6271

THE SCENE
Meg and Marco meet at this quaint locale for lunch. Meg uses anagrams to hint that she would like to get married. Marco tells Meg she is not ready.

BEHIND THE SCENE
Cafe Moka is one of 70 historic buildings in the Tavernier area. The building was home to The Key Theater circa 1932. Since then it has housed the Tavern Store as well as a series of restaurants including Old Tavernier and the Copper Kettle. Today, Cafe Moka is a breezy hangout serving French pastries, sandwiches and all types of coffee. They also have a decent selection of beer and wine.

GETTING THERE
The French style café is located at Mile Marker 91.8, Oceanside. Look for it at the corner of the Overseas Highway and Atlantic Circle Drive. They are open from 7AM to 5PM Sunday through Wednesday and from 7AM to 9PM Thursday through Saturday.

FIRST FEATURED
Part 6 | 48:40

NERD IS THE WORD
Enrique Murciano *(Detective Marco Diaz)* can recite Lamar's rap from *Revenge of the Nerds* in its entirety.

16

MARINERS HOSPITAL
91500 OVERSEAS HIGHWAY
TAVERNIER
FACEBOOK.COM/MARINERSHOSPITAL
(305) 434-3000

THE SCENE

Robert Rayburn is admitted to the hospital for head trauma. Tensions flare as his family tries to determine what happened to him. While gathered at the hospital, the family learns that Danny never left the Keys.

BEHIND THE SCENE

Founded in 1962, Mariners Hospital is a 25-bed inpatient critical access facility. Locals visit for more than medical attention by taking advantage of the excellent kitchen for lunch and joining the Wellness Center for workouts. Today Mariners is part of Baptist Health South Florida and one of three hospitals in the Keys. (Fisherman's Hospital is in Marathon and the Lower Keys Medical Center is found near Key West.)

GETTING THERE

Mariners Hospital is located at Mile Marker 91.5, Bayside. Mariners is open 24 hours.

FIRST FEATURED

Part 2 | 14:56

WRITE WRIGHT RIGHT

Sam Shepard *(Robert Rayburn)* is an American playwright and has authored 44 plays. He was once roommates with Charlie Mingus Jr., son of jazz great Charles Mingus.

17

PLANTATION KEY COURTHOUSE
88820 OVERSEAS HIGHWAY
TAVERNIER
(305) 292-3423

THE SCENE
Exterior shots taken at the Upper Keys courthouse include Meg talking to Prosecutor Karen about striking a deal for Carlos. Meg also runs into her former 'under the sheets' partner in crime, Alec, here. In this parking lot, they officially end their affair.

BEHIND THE SCENE
When locals are called to jury duty they are either assigned to the Plantation Key Courthouse or to Key West, some two hours south. The courthouse is a good example of a shooting location that requires little set design. Not much excitement here. Let's hope that checking out a Bloodline location is the only reason you will ever visit the courthouse!

GETTING THERE
Look for the white building near Mile Marker 88.8, Bayside. Slow down and turn when you smell the bureaucracy.

FIRST FEATURED
Part 6 | 24:36

MAD WOMAN
Linda Edna Cardellini *(Meg Rayburn)* received her first Emmy nomination for her portrayal of Sylvia Rosen, Don Draper's married mistress in *Mad Men*.

18

ISLAND HOME
88720 OVERSEAS HIGHWAY
TAVERNIER
(305) 852-4715

THE SCENE
John Rayburn's wife, Diana, manages a nursery. After causing friction between Diana and John, Danny shows up here and tries to clear the air with her. Though he starts out apologizing for causing any problems, by the end of the conversation Danny's apology starts to sounds more like a threat.

BEHIND THE SCENE
During filming of Season 1, the nursery was called the Gerry Droney Landscaping Nursery. It has since been sold to Allen Wood, owner of Forest Tek Lumber.

GETTING THERE
The nursery is located at Mile Marker 88.7, Bayside. Look for the plants and the white picket fence. Driving south along the Overseas Highway, the entrance to the nursery is located at the far side of the property.

FIRST FEATURED
Part 9 | 23:21

REAL WORLD
Jacinda Barrett *(Diana Rayburn)* is from Australia. She was first introduced to American audiences in 1992 on MTV's *Real World: London.*

19

MARLIN FOOD STORES

88601 OVERSEAS HIGHWAY
ISLAMORADA
(305) 852-6480

THE SCENE
Though Marlin's is not at Mile Marker 94 as shown on the show, this is the location where Carlos drops off some cocaine after Danny instructs him to fuel up at Mile Marker 94, Pump 2. Carlos pumps gas. A car pulls up next to him and they pop their trunk. Carlos places the red duffle bag of cocaine in their trunk and they drive away.

BEHIND THE SCENE
This is a cool local convenience store where you can fuel up cheaply. To create the best photographic opportunity, fill your vehicle up at Pump 2 and try not to act suspiciously if a police officer drives up.

GETTING THERE
As noted above, Marlin Food Stores is not actually at Mile Marker 94. The 24-hour gas station is found at Mile Marker 88.6, Oceanside. Look for the blue metal roof and gas pumps.

FIRST FEATURED
Part 9 | 15:28

ALL ABOUT THE BENJAMINS
Monroe County conducted a study on the economic impact of Bloodline. It estimated the Bloodline production impact and film-induced tourism brought in $158.7 million to the Keys.

20

TOM THUMB
88501 OVERSEAS HIGHWAY
ISLAMORADA
MYTOMTHUMB.COM | (305) 852-7242

THE SCENE
After Danny has gone missing, Kevin spots him at Tom Thumb putting gas in Chelsea's car. He calls John to let him know that he has seen Danny. Kevin flashes a gun as he approaches his brother. The gun is hidden in his waistband as he attempts to order Danny into his vehicle. Danny ignores his brother and walks away.

BEHIND THE SCENE
Tom Thumb is a national chain, as well as our neighborhood convenience store. You're probably going to stop for gas. Why not fill up where Danny did?

GETTING THERE
There are several Tom Thumb gas stations in the Keys. This one can be found at Mile Marker 88.5, Oceanside. Danny filled up at the outside pump closest to the southbound side of the highway.

FIRST FEATURED
Part 12 | 23:56

MIDDLE GROUND
Norbert Leo Butz uses his middle name so that people don't confuse him with his father, Norbert Butz. Best known for his work on Broadway, Leo is a two-time Tony Award winner.

21

MARKER 88
88000 OVERSEAS HIGHWAY
ISLAMORADA
MARKER88.INFO | (305) 852-9315

THE SCENE

When Danny and his father are seated at their bayside table for lunch, Danny is expecting his brothers to join them. In this scene, the rejection of his father breaks an already broken Danny. Father and son sit in a glider booth, and after asking the waitress if she would like to join them, Robert tells Danny to leave the Keys and offers him a check as a payout to do so. Danny tears up the check.

BEHIND THE SCENE

Marker 88 has been a Keys tradition since 1967. Located on a natural beach, they serve Florida seafood and prime steaks in an environment that is elegant but Keys casual. Many of the Bloodline cast and crew came to relax at Marker 88 when they were in the area shooting.

GETTING THERE

The location is the same as the name. Watch for the red and blue marker buoy. This iconic restaurant is found at Mile Marker 88, Bayside. Open every day from 11AM to 10PM, this is one of the premier sunset viewing locales in the Florida Keys.

FIRST FEATURED
Part 4 | 46:04

METAL HEART
An official *Bloodline* trailer included the Lissie cover of Metallica's *Nothing Else Matters*.

22

POSTNET
88005 OVERSEAS HIGHWAY
ISLAMORADA
POSTNET.COM/ISLAMORADA-FL105 | (305) 853-1101

THE SCENE
The PostNmail is the island shipping business where Danny goes to mail money made from his work stealing gas with Eric O'Bannon.

BEHIND THE SCENE
Called PostNet in real life, the post and ship store offers copying, shipping, and graphic design services. It is found on Plantation Key, named for the coconut and pineapple plantations once found here. Mail your postcards from here so you can brag to friends that they were mailed from the same place as Danny's dirty money.

GETTING THERE
PostNet is located in Plaza 88 at Mile Marker 88, Oceanside. They are open Monday through Friday from 9AM to 5PM. Closed Saturday and Sunday.

FIRST FEATURED
Part 3 | 16:20

DOWN UNDER
Series star Ben Mendelsohn *(Danny Rayburn)* is Australian. To develop his American accent, he worked with dialect coach Thom Jones to custom-tailor his speech patterns.

23

FOUNDERS PARK
87000 OVERSEAS HIGHWAY
ISLAMORADA
ISLAMORADA.FL.US/FOUNDERS_PARK.ASP
(305) 664-6400

THE SCENE

The Rayburn family gathers at this park in several episodes, including the high school baseball game, a beachside birthday party, and a swimming pool scene.

BEHIND THE SCENE

Local legend suggests that the property that was once the Plantation Key Yacht Harbor was purchased with Mob money. Today the 40 acres of green space known as Founders Park includes two baseball fields, soccer fields, fitness center, an Olympic swimming pool, a marina, tennis courts, and a sandy beach. The Home of the Hurricanes sign seen on the scoreboard in the baseball game episode refers to the Coral Shore High School Hurricanes who play here. In fact, it is the Coral Shores baseball team seen playing on Bloodline.

GETTING THERE

The park is open from 8AM to 6PM on weekdays and 10AM to 5PM on weekends. There is an $8 per person entry fee for non-Islamorada residents. The park can be found at Mile Marker 87, Bayside.

FIRST FEATURED

Part 4 | 15.51

PEOPLE ARE PEOPLE

In 2007, Enrique Murciano, who plays Detective Marco Diaz, came in at #7 on *People Magazine's* list of *The Sexiest Men Alive.*

24

SEASON 3 HIDEOUT
77522 OVERSEAS HIGHWAY
ISLAMORADA
ROBBIES.COM | (305) 664-8070

THE SCENE

Season 3 started filming just as this book was going to press, so we took out a location that was renovated beyond recognition and replaced it with a location where a lot of filming is taking place. The crew tells us one of the cast will be using this place as their hideout. We can probably guess who.

BEHIND THE SCENE

Behind the commercial area of Robbie's Marina is a community of liveaboard vessels, houseboats and trailers. The hideout is located here.

GETTING THERE

The hideout is can be seen by land or water at Robbie's.

FIRST FEATURED

Season 3

SEE IF IT STICKS

Florida Keys residents embraced Bloodline when it was filmed. "Rayburn for Sheriff" stickers are often seen on car bumpers or adorning the walls of bars in the Florida Keys.

HOG HEAVEN
85361 OVERSEAS HIGHWAY
ISLAMORADA
HOGHEAVENSPORTSBAR.COM | (305) 664-9669

THE SCENE
John Rayburn follows Ozzy into the parking lot of this oceanfront bar. When Ozzy parks his car and enters the bar, John breaks into Ozzy's car and steals his gun.

BEHIND THE SCENE
Hog Heaven is a popular sports bar and grill serving up lunch, dinner and cold drinks late into the night. Locals love the spot for live music.

GETTING THERE
Arrive by boat or by car. Hog Heaven is located at Mile Marker 85.3, Oceanside, near the foot of the Windley Key side of the Snake Creek Bridge. A huge sign marks the entrance. The bar is set back on the water behind an apartment building. They are open from 11AM to 3:30AM every day of the week.

FIRST FEATURED
Part 23 | 38:33

GATOR DONE
On shooting in the Florida Keys, co-creator Todd Kessler said, "There's very little infrastructure, crew, and space to actually film. What there is a lot of is mosquitoes and there can be alligators as well."

26

OCEANVIEW
INN & PUB
84500 OVERSEAS HIGHWAY
ISLAMORADA
THEOCEAN-VIEW.COM | (305) 664-8052

THE SCENE
Danny Rayburn's best friend, Eric, attempts to convince him that his family is no good for him while the two snort bumps of cocaine at this location. A fight ensues. Danny pushes Eric (and his chair) to the ground.

BEHIND THE SCENE
The OceanView Inn, locally referred to as the O.V., is owned by former Pittsburg Steeler and two-time Super Bowl champion Gary Dunn. The OceanView claims to have the oldest liquor license in the Florida Keys.

GETTING THERE
Islamorada's Windley Key is a small island known for fossil coral reefs, rumrunners, and Theater of the Sea, one of oldest marine mammal facilities in North America. Driving south on Windley Key, the OceanView is the first building on the Bayside of the highway. Cast and crew frequented the bar during off-production hours.

FIRST FEATURED
Part 1 | 43:55

CASTING CALL
The casting call for Eric O'Bannon described him as, "Long-haired, skinny, tattooed guy from the Keys." Actor Jamie McShane went into the audition thinking, "OK! I'm 0 for 4."

27

CAPTAIN
LARRY'S TRAIL
84500 OVERSEAS HIGHWAY
ISLAMORADA
THEOCEAN-VIEW.COM | (305) 664-8052

THE SCENE

Captain Larry's Trail begins behind the O.V. and cuts through the mangroves leading out to the bay. Legend suggests that the path is an old smuggler's trail. Whether or not that story holds any water, the view across Florida Bay from the walkway is breathtaking, and this is where Meg and Kevin discuss cutting Danny out of their parents' will while their father is in the hospital.

BEHIND THE SCENE

A lot of drug smuggling used to take place in the Florida Keys. Take a walk down Captain Larry's Trail and you will see why it was ideal for bringing in things that you didn't want people to know you were bringing in.

GETTING THERE

Grab a beer from the bar at OceanView and head towards the back of the parking lot by the bay. The trail is marked with Captain Larry's name and the walk through the mangroves will make you feel like smuggling something of your own.

FIRST FEATURED

Part 3 | 35:59

FORWARD THINKING

Bloodline is a partnership between Netflix and Sony Pictures Television. The partnership marks Netflix's first major deal with a film studio for a TV series.

28

ABEL'S TACKLE BOX
84341 OVERSEAS HIGHWAY
ISLAMORADA
(305) 664-2900

THE SCENE
When Danny is coming home to the Keys in Part 1, his brother John waits to pick him up at the Islamorada bus stop. When the bus arrives, John is waiting, but Danny never steps off the bus.

BEHIND THE SCENE
Not really a bus stop, Abel's Tackle Box and Deli is a great place to pick up bait, tackle, ice, beer and anything else you might need for a day on the water. If Patrick is around, you might pick up some fishing tips, too.

GETTING THERE
Abel's Tackle Box and Deli is located just south of Theater of the Sea at Mile Marker 84.3, Oceanside. Since the Bloodline filming, the building has been spruced up a bit.

FIRST FEATURED
Part 1 | 8:03

ALL IN THE FAMILY
Kyle Chandler *(John Rayburn)* was the first Rayburn sibling cast in the show. Ben Mendelsohn was the only actor the series met with for the role of Danny Rayburn.

29

JAWS RAW BAR
84001 OVERSEAS HIGHWAY
ISLAMORADA
HOLIDAYISLE.COM I (305) 664-2321

THE SCENE

When Kevin and Belle's marriage hits a rough patch, she turns to online dating. Belle meets a man identified as Foodie70 for a date at this Oceanside bar. She does not realize that her husband, Kevin, is at the bar spying on her.

BEHIND THE SCENE

The Postcard Inn has undergone a number of changes over the last few years. Once a Spring Break haven, the resort has made efforts to clean up its image and its hotel rooms. The property is home to several bars, so a cold drink and some Florida Keys fare are never too far away.

GETTING THERE

It is hard to miss The Postcard Inn at Mile Marker 84, Oceanside. The Raw Bar is right on the ocean, so head to the water. The Raw Bar is open from 11AM to 9PM Sunday through Thursday and 11AM to 11PM on weekends. Be sure to check out the Tiki Bar here too. It's another film location.

FIRST FEATURED

Part 6 | 30:35

SAVED BY THE BELLE

Katie Finneran's *(Belle Rayburn)* jobs when she first started acting included ringside girl at a boxing ring and perfume spray girl at Bloomingdale's.

30

THE TIKI BAR
84001 OVERSEAS HIGHWAY
ISLAMORADA
HOLIDAYISLE.COM | (305) 664-2321

THE SCENE
While sipping cocktails at the Tiki Bar, Kevin bumps into his brother Danny's sort-of-girlfriend Chelsea. After they throw back a few drinks and commiserate about their problems, including the topic of the price of an online divorce, they further complicate their separate situations by sleeping together.

BEHIND THE SCENE
This bar opened in 1969 as The Hapi Hula Hut. In 1971 it was named The Tiki Bar and in 1972 the owner challenged his bartender, Tiki John, to concoct a cocktail using some of the overstocked bar liquors and liqueurs. The end result was the birth of the rumrunner. Though the bar closed while it underwent a freshening, the World Famous Tiki Bar reopened in the summer of 2016.

GETTING THERE
Turn off at The Postcard Inn when you reach Mile Marker 84, Oceanside. The Tiki Bar is located on the far side of the resort's marina.

FIRST FEATURED
Part 6 | 50:38

SWEET & SASSY
Chloë Stevens Sevigny *(Chelsea O'Bannon)* was discovered on the street by a fashion editor for Sassy magazine. She is known for choosing roles with a good script over roles offering a big paycheck.

31

WHALE HARBOR
83413 OVERSEAS HIGHWAY
ISLAMORADA

THE SCENE

When Sarah Rayburn drowns while trying to retrieve her seahorse necklace, the location was named as Whale Harbor. Sarah's drowning factors strongly into many of the Rayburn family dramas.

BEHIND THE SCENE

Though not an actual filming location, Whale Harbor includes a channel, a bridge, a restaurant, and a marina. To sit back and soak in some of the local vibrations, have a seat at the outside bar at Wahoo's Restaurant, sip on a cold beer, and stare out at the murderous Atlantic waters.

GETTING THERE

Whale Harbor is located at Mile Marker 83.4, Oceanside. The large parking lot and marina are located at the foot of the Upper Matecumbe side of the Whale Harbor Bridge. For decades this was home to the iconic though decorative Whale Harbor lighthouse.

FIRST FEATURED

Referenced only

BEFORE & AFTER

Young Sarah is portrayed by Angela Winiewicz. Mia Kirshner plays the more mature 'Ghost Sarah,' seen talking to Danny on his bus ride to the Keys.

32

TINY'S BAIT
82788 OVERSEAS HIGHWAY
ISLAMORADA
(305) 414-8346

THE SCENE

Rafi Quintana cranks the music up in his red Pontiac G6 while sitting in the parking lot of this gas station. He reactivates his cell phone and calls Danny. The DEA is tracking the phone, and so they figure out his location.

BEHIND THE SCENE

Tiny's is family owned and known for their friendly service and reasonable prices. They offer gas, cold beer and frozen bait. It is a local favorite. Turn up your music and enjoy.

GETTING THERE

In the show they say Rafi is at the corner of Palm Avenue and Highway 1, but Tiny's is actually located at the corner of De Leon Avenue and the Overseas Highway at Mile Marker 82.8, Bayside. Watch for their blue and white sign and the blue roof over the gas pumps.

FIRST FEATURED

Part 10 | 52:20

ROCK & ROLE

Gino Vento *(Rafi Quintana)* is the former vocalist of the hardcore band Thick As Blood. The band's guitarist, Randy Gonzalez, also appears in the show as Manny.

33

BILL'S CUSTOM
AUTOMOTIVE
82760 OVERSEAS HIGHWAY
ISLAMORADA
(305) 664-4531

THE SCENE
After finding a dead girl in the water, John Rayburn and Detective Marco Diaz travel to a local garage to show a picture of the victim to one of the mechanics. The mechanic, Vicente Cruz, recognizes the girl in the picture and begins to cry. The relationship between Vincente and the dead girl gives the officers a new lead in the case.

BEHIND THE SCENE
Bill Ismer is the Bill in Bill's Auto, the site of a former Texaco station. Bill also owns the tiki wood art shop next door. Should work be required on your vehicle, Bill's is locally trusted.

GETTING THERE
Watch for the blue roofed garage at Mile Marker 82.7, Oceanside. You'll miss this one if you allow yourself to be distracted by the ship shaped building on the other side of the road or the wood sculpture shop next door. These guys are here to work on cars, so pop in for an oil change or check out this location on a drive by.

FIRST FEATURED
Part 8 | 9:01

HEAVY MEDAL
Chaz Mena *(Vicente Cruz)* won the Freedom Foundation's "George Washington Honor Medal" in 2014 for his one-person play. It garnered him Congressional Recognition.

34

THE WHISTLE STOP
82685 OVERSEAS HIGHWAY
ISLAMORADA
KEYSDINING.COM/WP/ | (305) 664-0094

THE SCENE

Danny seems to frequent this long-standing local dive, as multiple scenes have been shot at this location. Danny has been seen at the Whistle Stop drinking, fighting, and at one point in a particularly drunken display, walking out of the front door and peeing on the side of the building.

BEHIND THE SCENE

The Whistle Stop offers a full bar, pool tables, TV's and your typical pub grub. It has the vibe of a local watering hole and plenty of local color. Plus, it's a great place to shoot pool on the same table where Danny played!

GETTING THERE

Located at Mile Marker 82.6, Oceanside, the Whistle Stop can be found directly opposite the red train caboose on the other side of the highway. Look for the round sign advertising Subway and Sub Zero ice cream. The Whistle Stop is open every day of the week from 12PM to 3AM.

FIRST FEATURED

Part 6 | 11:32

I'M ON A BOAT

Ben Mendelsohn describes the Florida Keys as a beautiful holiday spot and a paradise. His advice: "Make sure you go out on a boat because that is when the Florida Keys really comes into its own."

MANGROVE MIKE'S
82200 OVERSEAS HIGHWAY
ISLAMORADA
MANGROVEMIKES.COM | (305) 664-8022

THE SCENE
After the death of his father, Danny meets Chelsea and they discuss his future plans. When Danny sees Detective Lenny Potts, he gets spooked and complains that his eggs are not over-easy, and rushes out without paying his bill.

BEHIND THE SCENE
Mangrove Mike's is the local favorite greasy spoon serving damn fine diner fare. It has been voted "Islamorada's Best Breakfast Place" since 1998. Grab a seat at the counter like Danny and Chelsea did. Be sure to save room for the Key lime pie.

GETTING THERE
Located adjacent to the funky Sunset Inn at Mile Marker 82.2, Bayside. Mangrove Mike's is open from 6AM to 2PM seven days a week.

FIRST FEATURED
Part 5 | 12:26

BINGE WORTHY
Show-runner described the first season of Bloodline as a 13-hour saga designed for Netflix's 'binge-watch' model.

36

THE ISLANDER,
A GUY HARVEY OUTPOST
82100 OVERSEAS HIGHWAY
ISLAMORADA
GUYHARVEYOUTPOSTISLAMORADA.COM
(305) 664-2031

THE SCENE

From the very first episode there is talk about the Rayburn Pier. When Danny departs the bus on his way home, the pier is talked about on the front page of the *Island Gazette*. This is one of the reasons Danny chooses now for his homecoming — at least it proves an excellent excuse. When the community gathers for the dedication of the pier, Sally Rayburn delivers a speech.

BEHIND THE SCENE

The Rayburn Pier scene was filmed at The Islander Resort, a Guy Harvey Outpost. During filming of the scene, extras were kept cool in the Islander's Conference Center, designed by Bruce Merenda. (Mr. Merenda also designed St. Petersburg's Salvador Dali Museum.) The Conference Center provides two services for The Islander Resort: it provides a place for weddings and corporate meetings, and also serves as home to the Keys History & Discovery Center.

GETTING THERE

The unmistakable retro Islander sign has been visible from the highway since the 1950s at Mile Marker 82, Oceanside. The pier is located at the back of the resort on the water.

FIRST FEATURED

Part 10 | 1:27

VENDOR BENDER

During the filming of Season 1, Bloodline production engaged over 600 vendors in the state of Florida.

37

CORAL BAY MARINA
601 MASTIC STREET
ISLAMORADA
CORAL-BAY-MARINA.COM | (305) 664-3111

THE SCENE
Called Indian Key Channel Marina in the series, this business is known to locals as Coral Bay Marina. Fans of the show know it as Kevin Rayburn's marina and office, where he can be seen snorting lots of cocaine and generally melting down. This is also the site where Kevin and Danny work to restore their father's old Chevy truck in Season 1.

BEHIND THE SCENE
Coral Bay is a full service, working marina established in 1983. They have 30+ wet slips for transient and live-aboard customers and onsite mechanics for all types of boat services.

GETTING THERE
The marina is open Monday through Friday from 8AM to 4:30PM, and 7AM to 3:30PM in the summer. This is a working marina. Consider parking in the parking lot of the family owned Trading Post, open 24 hours, at Mile Marker 82, Bayside. Belle's Boutique is located here, as is a restaurant frequented by cast and crew, Bad Boy Burrito. You can usually cut to the marina through the rear fence.

FIRST FEATURED
Featured often.

38

TACKLE CENTER OF ISLAMORADA
81924 OVERSEAS HIGHWAY
ISLAMORADA
TACKLECENTERISLAMORADA.COM
(305) 664-9800

THE SCENE

Welcome to Wayne Lowry's tackle shop. This location is featured in several scenes – in the first, Danny follows Eric's crime connection here and ends up with a gun drawn on him. John and the DEA know that Lowry is up to no good, but through Season 1, are unable to find any proof. Authorities keep the tackle shop under observation hoping Lowry will eventually slip up.

BEHIND THE SCENE

The Tackle Center of Islamorada has everything you could need when it comes to bait and tackle. Non-anglers can stop in for a cap or t-shirt. This is the premier tackle center in the Florida Keys.

GETTING THERE

Look for the red bait sign at Mile Marker 81.9, Bayside. The shop is located in close proximity to the excellent sunset bar, Lorelei. To find Lorelei just look for the giant mermaid posing on the side of the road. The tackle shop opens at 5:30AM, seven days a week.

FIRST FEATURED

Part 7 | 41:35

ON TREK

Glenn Morshower *(Wayne Lowry)* changed his name from "Morchower" for his acting career. He has had guest roles in *Star Trek: The Next Generation, Star Trek: Voyager* and *Star Trek: Enterprise.*

39

MISS MONROE
81868 OVERSEAS HIGHWAY
ISLAMORADA
WWW.SHOPMISSMONROE.COM | (305) 440-3951

THE SCENE

Kevin Rayburn's wife Belle works at this local boutique. Kevin comes into the store to see his wife and she tells him she just sold expensive jewelry to someone in real estate. Belle makes sure to tell them about Kevin and his marina.

BEHIND THE SCENE

Miss Monroe is a fun, beachy, boutique with a great selection of jewelry, sun hats, and cover-ups. They also sell "Rayburn for Sheriff" and "Rayburn House" shirts. Liz and Sam Huddleston opened Miss Monroe in 2012.

GETTING THERE

A bit tricky to find, but worth the effort. Miss Monroe is located at the Village Square, a funky little shopping area accessible from the parking lot of the Trading Post at Mile Marker 81.8, Bayside. After purchasing your own Rayburn for Sheriff T-shirt, stay for the best Mexican food in Islamorada at Bad Boy Burrito. Kevin's Marina is on the other side of the wooden fence here.

FIRST FEATURED

Part 15 | 13:00

SOUND ADVICE

When not filming on location in the Florida Keys, Bloodline production utilized a warehouse sound stage in Homestead, Florida for interior shots.

40

ATLANTIC'S EDGE
81801 OVERSEAS HIGHWAY
ISLAMORADA
CHEECA.COM | (305) 712-7126

THE SCENE

When Danny and his mother go out for a quiet dinner, Danny, a former chef, asks if Sally would be interested in opening the Rayburn House restaurant to the public. Sally replies, "No more business talk today. I'm having dinner with my son."

BEHIND THE SCENE

This fine dining restaurant is located on the edge of the Atlantic Ocean in the exclusive Cheeca Lodge. The property boasts the longest pier in the Keys and was a favorite stop for President George H.W. Bush when he visited. Long before this was a resort property, it was home to the Matecumbe community's grammar school, a Methodist Church, and a pioneer graveyard. The graveyard is still located on the property.

GETTING THERE

Located at Mile Marker 81.8, Oceanside, the Cheeca Lodge Resort & Spa is a private, upscale resort. Reservations are required, so be sure to call ahead.

FIRST FEATURED

Part 9 | 12:11

ROYAL TREATMENT

Sissy Spacek *(Sally Rayburn)* is the 22nd great granddaughter of King Edward I. Her cousin, Rip Torn, convinced her not to change her name for acting.

41

PHOTO: ANCHORED MEDIA

MOORINGS VILLAGE
123 BEACH ROAD
ISLAMORADA
THEMOORINGSVILLAGE.COM | (305) 664-4708

THE SCENE

The waterfront hotel owned by Robert and Sally Rayburn is featured regularly, hosting everything from a funeral to a family reunion.

BEHIND THE SCENE

The property was originally home to the Matecumbe Club, constructed in 1919 for the exclusive use of 11 members of the New York Cotton Exchange. The Club was destroyed in the 1935 Labor Day Hurricane; reconstruction began in 1936 with the building of a private residence and several outlying buildings. The area was devastated again by Hurricane Donna in 1960. Ralph Edsell, Sr., re-developed the property, constructing a small beachside resort. The property was upgraded in the late 1980s with the addition of 14 cottages.

GETTING THERE

The property is only accessible to guests of the resort. If you are not a guest, save yourself the trouble of being turned away without having seen anything. Instead, rent a paddleboard or kayak from Cheeca Lodge, paddle by, and check out the great view of the property from the water.

FIRST FEATURED

Multiple episodes. Primary set.

SLEEP LIKE THE RAYBURNS

The Blue Charlotte House, home to the Rayburn clan, is a three bedroom, 6500 square foot home at Moorings Village available for about $2500 per night.

42

PIERRE'S
81600 OVERSEAS HIGHWAY
ISLAMORADA
MORADABAY.COM/PIERRES | (305) 664-3225

THE SCENE
Larry asks John Rayburn to meet him at this upscale restaurant four days after Danny's murder. John is told that he is on the short list of candidates to become the next sheriff.

BEHIND THE SCENE
Pierre's opened in 1999 and offers fine dining with French fusion cuisine and cocktails in a colonial style residence. Zagat's calls Pierre's one of the top all-around dining experiences in the Florida Keys. The sunset views are exquisite.

GETTING THERE
Pierre's has a casual elegance dress code. Jacket and tie are not required, but reservations are. Watch for their sign at Mile Marker 81.6, Bayside. Pierre's shares a beach and parking lot with a sister restaurant — Morada Beach Cafe — another Bloodline film location.

FIRST FEATURED
Part 13 | 2:21

FLYING COACH
Kyle Chandler took the role of John Rayburn, in part, so that people would not always think of him as Coach Taylor from *Friday Night Lights*.

43

MORADA BAY
BEACH CAFE
81600 OVERSEAS HIGHWAY
ISLAMORADA
MORADABAY.COM | (305) 664-0604

THE SCENE

When Danny tells his brother he is going to Key West, he never makes the drive to the Southernmost City. Instead he stops at a beachside rave. He sits at the bar, drinking and smoking, while a younger crowd dances behind him. A sexy redhead approaches him and they snort cocaine in the bathroom before kissing on the dance floor. When the drugs run out, she leaves. Sally, Meg and Diana have coffee here in Part 11.

BEHIND THE SCENE

The Beach Cafe was designed to feel like a place where Hawaiian and Californian surfers would relax after a day on the water. The Full Moon Party they host is legendary, but the sunset views are the reason people stop here for a bite to eat and a cold drink.

GETTING THERE

The Cafe and the bar are open seven days a week, usually until at least 11:30PM. Watch for their sign at Mile Marker 81.6, Bayside. Morada Bay Beach Cafe shares a beach and a parking lot with Pierre's — another Bloodline film location.

FIRST FEATURED

Part 6 | 22:17

44

GREEN TURTLE INN
81219 OVERSEAS HIGHWAY
ISLAMORADA
GREENTURTLEINN.COM | (305) 664-2006

THE SCENE

Meg meets Marco at the Green Turtle and the two talk about moving to New York. When she confesses to an affair, Marco gets up from the table and walks out.

BEHIND THE SCENE

Originally home to the Rustic Inn, a reported speakeasy during the Prohibition years, the building was destroyed in the horrific 1935 Labor Day Hurricane. Rebuilt and reopened as Sid and Roxie's Green Turtle Inn in 1947, there was a time when 200-500 turtles were processed in their turtle cannery every week. Famous visitors include Ted Williams, Joe Namath, Mickey Mantle, Gilda Radnor, and John Belushi. The current structure was built in 2004 on the footprint of Sid and Roxie's place.

GETTING THERE

Located at Mile Marker 81, Oceanside, look for the iconic Sid and Roxie's neon sign. Open Tuesday through Sunday for breakfast, lunch and dinner. The Turtle rests on Monday.

FIRST FEATURED

Part 10 | 13:34

COME ON DOWN

Linda Cardellini *(Meg Rayburn)* was a contestant in a 1994 episode of *The Price Is Right*. She won a fireplace.

45

(OO-TRAY)
80939 OVERSEAS HIGHWAY
ISLAMORADA
OO-TRAY.COM | (305) 922-2027

THE SCENE

No interior shots were filmed at this whiskey bar and restaurant, but the exterior is visible in several scenes. In one, an angry Kevin takes the untraceable gun and drives the Overseas Highway looking for Danny. He spots the old Chevy pickup that Danny drives parked in the oo-tray parking lot.

BEHIND THE SCENE

oo-tray is a restaurant with local farm to table flavor and is known locally as the place to go for whiskey. The French word "outre" (pronounced oo-tray) means unconventional, eccentric, or bizarre.

GETTING THERE

Located at Mile Marker 80.9, Oceanside, long time visitors to the Keys might remember this locale as home to Uncle's Restaurant. oo-tray is easy to spot with its distinctive sign and awning. They serve lunch from 11AM to 4PM, and dinner from 5PM to 11:30PM. The bar stays open until 1AM Thursday through Saturday.

FIRST FEATURED

Part 12 | 9:15

HOWDY NEIGHBOR

John Rayburn's house is found down a private road across the highway from oo-tray. oo-tray can be seen in the background as Danny drops John's kids off at the house.

46

ROBBIE'S
77522 OVERSEAS HIGHWAY
ISLAMORADA
ROBBIES.COM | (305) 664-8070

THE SCENE

Instead of meeting his brother when he gets to town, Danny meets his friend Eric O'Bannon at Robbie's where the two are seen relaxing in a small boat and smoking a joint. Between puffs, Eric offers Danny some shady employment.

BEHIND THE SCENE

Robbie's is a favorite joint in the Keys thanks to their popular tarpon feeding docks. You'll also find food, drink, art, boat rentals, and more than a few hungry pelicans. They also offer some of the best kayaking in the Florida Keys.

GETTING THERE

Watch for the service road off of the Overseas Highway just south of the Lignumvitae Bridge, Bayside near mile marker 77. Take the service road north and watch for the hustle and bustle. Parking is free. Beers are ice cold by the tarpon docks.

FIRST FEATURED

Part 1 | 11:21

FAMILY REUNION

Bloodline reunites actors Sam Shepard, Glen Morshower, and Enrique Murciano. They all starred in Blackhawk Down.

47

SAFARI LOUNGE
73814 OVERSEAS HIGHWAY
ISLAMORADA
(305) 664-8142

THE SCENE

John Rayburn is the serious brother, but Danny convinces him to relax a little and takes John drinking at this local favorite dive bar. They embark on a bender and discuss each other's faults and then they drink shots. John gives smoking a try. Danny gets a pretty girl's phone number for John. John throws up in the parking lot.

BEHIND THE SCENE

The official name of the bar is the Safari Lounge. Once known as the Dead Animal Bar for all the trophy heads mounted on its walls, it is simply referred to as The D.A.B. by locals today. The bathrooms of this oceanfront establishment are marked Tarzan and Jane.

GETTING THERE

It's very easy to find the Safari Lounge — just drive to Lower Matecumbe and look for the rhinoceros on the side of the road at Mile Marker 73.8, Oceanside. This is the only roadside rhinoceros you will find in the Keys, so don't second-guess yourself. The bar is open from 12PM to 12AM every day.

FIRST FEATURED

Part 8 | 33:34

TERROR ATTACK

"John is so terrorized by his own conscience. He has been his entire life, and Danny has been a big part of that."

— Linda Cardellini *(Meg Rayburn)* on the character of Rayburn brothers John and Danny.

48

HABANOS
OCEANFRONT
73510 OVERSEAS HIGHWAY
ISLAMORADA
(305) 517-6313

THE SCENE

This location was used for exterior shots of the place where Meg meets with Ozzy and pays him to keep quiet with the information he has on the Rayburn family. After handing him an envelope of money she tells Ozzy to "leave town, or else."

BEHIND THE SCENE

Good food served at a reasonable price, Habanos offers classic Cuban cooking in a low-key and casual oceanfront setting.

GETTING THERE

Habanos, found at Mile Marker 73.5, Oceanside, is open from 11AM to10PM six days a week. It is closed on Mondays.

FIRST FEATURED

Part 21 | 41:39

SOMETHING FISHY

One of Linda Cardellini's great experiences in the Florida Keys was feeding the tarpon at Robbie's Marina. Robbie's is a true roadside attraction, and she described the experience as both terrifying and exhilarating.

49

ANNE'S BEACH
MILE MARKER 73.5
ISLAMORADA
ANNESBEACH.COM

THE SCENE

Anne's Beach is the location where Robert Rayburn is kayaking when he sees Danny on the shore. The events that follow send Robert to the hospital.

BEHIND THE SCENE

Named after local environmentalist Anne Eaton, the waters are too shallow for swimming, but ideal for wading or kayaking. Don't pass up a stroll along the boardwalk. The beach is dog friendly, so feel free to bring your pup if it is a fan of the show. Lonely Planet named Anne's one of The Best Hidden Beaches in South Florida.

GETTING THERE

Anne's Beach is located close to Mile Marker 73, Oceanside, on Lower Matecumbe Key. The beach is open from sunrise to sunset. There are two parking lots that fill early. Bring your bug spray!

FIRST FEATURED

Part 2 | 13:37

KEYS DISEASE

Initially, only exterior shots were to be filmed in The Florida Keys while interior shots would be filmed in Georgia. The Keys locations became such a big part of the story that the show ended up filming almost entirely in the Keys.

50

LONG KEY
STATE PARK
67400 OVERSEAS HIGHWAY
LAYTON
FLORIDASTATEPARKS.ORG | (305) 664-4815

THE SCENE

The picturesque beach at the state park is where the tension between brothers Danny and John comes to a head. When they first meet, the two sit on a log and talk. The discussion escalates, fatally, with John eventually drowning his brother in the shallow water.

BEHIND THE SCENE

Long Key State Park is famous for its flats fishing. The state park boasts 60 oceanfront campsites for overnight stays, as well as fishing, hiking, swimming, and bird watching for day trippers.

GETTING THERE

The park is open from 8AM until sunset. Single admission is $4.50. Multiple person admission is $5 for the first person plus $0.50 per additional person. Campsites are $43 per night. Watch for the unassuming state park sign at Mile Marker 67.4, Oceanside. Take a right after the ranger booth and park near the kayaks. Follow the trail behind the kayaks for a couple hundred feet and you will find the area where the famous scene was filmed.

FIRST FEATURED
Part 12 | 45:50

HOT & COLD

Ben Mendelsohn described the beach scene as a tough shoot that took a couple of days. The sun was hot, but the water was cold. "It was sort of like the elements come up and give you a kick and say 'Ha ha ha! Enjoy this!' he said.

EAT

DRINK

SLEEP

REFUEL

RELAX

SHOP

HOT SPOTS TOUR 1

2
SNAP A PIC IN FRONT OF THE BLOODLINE BUS STOP.

3
GRAB A BEER AT DANNY'S TACO JOINT,
ALABAMA JACK'S.

6
DRIVE BY CASA O'BANNON TO SEE THE HOUSE
WHERE CHELSEA AND ERIC LIVED.

19
FUEL UP WHERE A DRUG DEAL WENT DOWN
AT MARLIN FOOD STORES.

31
DRIVE OVER TO WHALE HARBOR WHERE SARAH
DROWNED.

34
GRAB A BITE AT DANNY'S FAVORITE BAR,
THE WHISTLE STOP.

36
SEE THE RAYBURN PIER AT THE ISLANDER.

41
KAYAK BY THE RAYBURN HOUSE AT
MOORINGS VILLAGE RESORT.

HOT SPOTS TOUR 2

5
SEE WHERE A BODY WASHED UP
AT JEWFISH CREEK BRIDGE.

12
DRIVE BY DANNY'S HIDEOUT
AT STONE LEDGE PARADISE INN.

20
GET GAS WHERE DANNY WAS
THREATENED AT TOM THUMB.

26
GRAB LUNCH AT A BLOODLINE CAST AND CREW
FAVORITE,
THE OCEANVIEW.

27
WALK CAPTAIN LARRY'S TRAIL WHERE
RAYBURN SIBLINGS CONSPIRED.

37
SWING BY KEVIN'S BOATYARD AT CORAL BAY MARINA.

39
GRAB A RAYBURN SOUVENIR AT
BELLE'S BOUTIQUE, MISS MONROE.

50
SEE WHERE DANNY WAS MURDERED
AT LONG KEY STATE PARK.

HOT SPOTS TOUR 3

AUTHORS

BRAD BERTELLI

Brad Bertelli is the curator/historian at Islamorada's Keys History & Discovery Center. He has published four books on Florida and Florida Keys history, and operates Historic Upper Keys Walking Tours. His bi-weekly column, Notes on Keys History, appears in The Reporter.

Contact: brad@bradbertelli.com

DAVID SLOAN

David Sloan moved to the Florida Keys in 1996. He is the author of 18 books including *Quit Your Job and Move to Key West* and *The Key West Bucket List*. Sloan also runs the popular ghost tour and ghost hunt company, Haunted Key West, and co-produces the Key Lime Festival and the Zero K Cow Key Channel Bridge Run.

Contact david@phantompress.com

Made in the USA
Charleston, SC
28 February 2017

Please
Save me

Please Save me

One woman's battle for love and hope after
horrific abuse by her father

MANDY YOUSAF
WITH LINDA WATSON-BROWN

First published in the UK by John Blake Publishing
An imprint of The Zaffre Publishing Group
A Bonnier Books UK company
4th Floor, Victoria House
Bloomsbury Square,
London, WC1B 4DA
England

Owned by Bonnier Books
Sveavägen 56, Stockholm, Sweden

Paperback – 9781789467840
eBook – 9781789467857

A CIP catalogue of this book is available from the British Library.

Designed by Envy Design Ltd
Printed and bound by in Great Britain by Clays Ltd, Elcograf S.p.A

5 7 9 10 8 6 4

This book is a work of non-fiction, based on the life, experiences and recollections
of Mandy Yousaf. Certain details in this story, including names and locations, have
been changed to protect the identity and privacy of the authors, their family
and those mentioned.

John Blake Publishing is an imprint of Bonnier Books UK
www.bonnierbooks.co.uk

*To my Charlotte – and for everyone who feels
they don't have a voice x*

Contents

Foreword by Sammy Woodhouse

Mandy is an incredibly strong woman whose voice deserves to be heard by anyone who is appalled, as I am, by the way so many survivors of abuse are treated. She was the first mum that I spoke with about my own experience of conceiving a child through rape, and helped me enormously with my own personal journey. Mandy's story should be a wake-up call to those who turn a blind eye to the epidemic of child abuse across the globe – she is an absolute warrior.

Sammy Woodhouse
Author of *Just a Child* and campaigner

Prologue

I wish I could see stars when I look out of my bed at night. There's too much competition from the streetlamps, too much light pollution and not even any real darkness at all. It never gets properly dark, there's always a glow. If I could see the stars, I could count them – and if I could count them, I'd have something to focus on, something to distract me. I'd like that, I'd like a way of disappearing from where I am, of being transported to somewhere else, where everything was just as I'd want it to be, where I felt safe, where I felt loved.

Instead of counting stars, I count steps. Here they come. Here *he* comes.

It must be Monday.

Or Wednesday.

Or Friday.

Or Sunday.

He isn't even trying to keep quiet and he isn't creeping in, he's just solidly making his way to my room, where I'll be lying, waiting. I know what will happen because it's a pattern now. He has his nights, they never change, and he has what he does to me.

He's climbing in beside me and, the worst of it is, I don't fight, I don't argue, because I know that wouldn't change a single thing. There's nothing I can do to stop this because it's what he wants, and what he wants, he gets.

There he is and I'll just have to get through it, with no stars to count, nothing to hope for other than someone, someday, might notice. It's that someone I try to think of as he does the terrible things that he does to me. Maybe they will see the bruises. Maybe they will see that I'm terrified of him. Maybe they will see the child who is treated like a woman.

Please save me, I beg in my mind as his hands crawl over me, his body pushes into mine. *Please save me* … because I can't bear my father doing this to me any longer.

1

A Perfectly Normal Family

I don't remember much of my childhood – at least not until I was 11, not until *it* started.

Maybe I've blocked things out or maybe there just isn't that much to remember but 11 is where *it* began for me. My childhood wasn't an exciting time – there were no adventures, no fancy holidays, no amazing memories made that would last a lifetime. It was all quite boring really and there wasn't even a fascinating backstory to our family to make up for it.

We were normal.

A perfectly normal family.

I was born in October 1966 and my given name is Manda – hardly anyone has ever got that right and every official document, record or file about me calls me 'Amanda'. It was always Mandy anyway. We lived in

Halifax, West Yorkshire, and I'm the eldest of three girls, although we aren't close – looking at it all now, I don't see how we ever could have been. I lived in hell and why would anyone want to remind themselves of living through something like that?

There isn't that much at all to my early years. Some people know how their parents met, what their wedding was like, how they felt when they had their first baby; I have none of that. I've pieced a few bits together but it's not much. My memory comes and goes in waves. I know I've blocked a lot of it out (even the stuff before *it* was the biggest part of my life) and the jigsaw is missing so many pieces. It's frustrating, but it's also a way to protect myself. If I knew everything, would I even be able to face what my childhood was truly like?

Mum – Jenny – was young when she got together with Dad, only 16 or so from what I can work out. He wasn't much older, not yet 20, and neither of them had amounted to anything by the time they got together, and they never would. Mum's parents, my gram and grandad, weren't the type to show any affection but I know they loved me. There were no hugs, they didn't give me words of love, but they were good grandparents. There were always sweets and little gifts from Gram Mildred and even though I don't know anything about Mum's childhood, I've never seen or heard anything to suggest they would have been any different with her. They were good people who just happened to have a daughter who seemingly had no interest in being a decent mother. Who knows why that was – I don't know their entire story, I don't know whether my father identified and groomed Mum as being someone who would go along with what he would later do, all I can say is that she was never the mother she should have been, she never protected me and I never felt love from her.

I do know that Mum started drinking at a very young age and her parents didn't approve of that, but they certainly didn't keep their distance from her or go on about it when we were there: they were just decent. I went to them for tea a lot and often stayed over; it was a place where I felt safe and I knew that Gram would always be there with a little treat for me whenever I visited. She was my safe haven – just a little old grandmother, who always had a pinny on and was always working. She'd get up at five in the morning to go to a cleaning job then she'd come home, clean the house and cook, then go out once more to clean nightclubs and bars again. She worked so hard but never complained about it. I was her favourite for years, I knew that, and I loved it, and I also feel that I lit up her life of drudgery whenever we were together.

I don't remember Mum having any friends and she wasn't close to her only sister – she kept herself to herself. She was always dressed in the style of the time: short skirts or dresses, moving on to trousers as the 1970s went on, with a jet-black dyed beehive hairdo. Mum was slim and quite pretty, but her whole identity was based around being seen as a traditional mother and housewife, even though she wasn't actually like that at all. Drinking played such a big part of her life that nothing else mattered as much. Every now and then she went to the bingo with Gram, she did a bit of shopping for herself, but there is very little to grab onto and think, *that's my mum, that's who she was.*

Dad – Keith Meadows – was from Halifax, just like Mum, but his parents were different as they were members of The Salvation Army, the Protestant church charity. A lot of people might think of the 'Sally Ann' as the group most visible singing Christmas carols or working with the homeless – and it's true they do a great deal of good with the latter – but they also impose a lot of restrictions. They abstain from alcohol, tobacco, the non-medical use of addictive drugs, gambling, pornography, the occult and what they describe as anything that can 'enslave the body or spirit'. Dad was brought up with all of that as a big influence in his life, and his parents were strict with us grandchildren because of it, and I'd imagine they were the same with him and his siblings. I often saw them dressed in their uniforms – they were in the band (Dad played the trumpet) and they always seemed to be on marches. They performed outside of hospitals and they hung around when it was chucking-out time in the local pubs, always trying to sell their magazine, *The War Cry*, always trying to find what they called 'soldiers' (fellow disciples). They had committed themselves to God and were very much against alcohol, which meant they had no time for my mum. Dad left The Salvation Army for a time as I don't remember seeing him in his uniform for a while when I was growing up, but he would be dragged back into it in later years: he loved the attention he got when he was dressed up, the camaraderie from other disciples, and I think also the notion that he must be a moral man because of his pledge to the cause.

Those grandparents, his mum and dad – Cyril and Irene – were horrible. They weren't loving at all; unlike my mum's parents, they showed no caring side whatsoever. They didn't show *love* in any way. The best way I can describe it is that they always seemed 'off' with me – there was no warmth in any shape or form, they were very cold people and never really engaged with me, their granddaughter. We did sometimes go to their caravan when they allowed it, but those weren't particularly happy times – they've just passed into the general blur of my childhood.

I've no idea how Mum and Dad met. He worked in a cloth factory when he was younger and she worked in a sweet factory; maybe there's something there but I was never told if that was how it came about. Also, I have no idea how they felt about having me as a baby – there were no stories about it and it seemed neither of them really engaged with me. Neither of them ever said that they were delighted to find out Mum was pregnant or that they were nervous about how they would look after their first child. She was only 16 and he wasn't much older at 18, but I have no idea if they were nervous or made plans, if they felt too young to be starting a family or whether it seemed like the right time for them. I don't know what I looked like when I was born, when I took my first steps, what my first words were, whether I liked dolls or teddies. There isn't a single story about me as a baby or little girl which came to me through them, there are no family photos, no grainy images of me as a baby in their arms, nothing at all that comes from being in a 'normal' family. When I think of it, it seems so odd. My kids know everything about how me and their dad met, they know about how they were as babies, they have a world of stories that tell them who they are – I have nothing.

Mum cooked, cleaned, kept house, drank – and that was it. I don't remember her ever saying she loved me. She never played with me, she just pottered about the house and only had jobs sporadically. To me the strange thing is that she would only have been a teenager when I was born and when she lived that way, yet she had signed her whole existence away to a life of drudgery and unhappiness from such an early age. I can't imagine her as someone full of life, as a young woman with hopes and dreams. She never expressed any joy or seemed happy unless she was drunk. By the time she had her next baby, when I was six, she was still only in her early twenties, which is nothing really, certainly far too young to have such a dreary life, never looking forward to anything but the next bottle of booze.

The day my sister was born is probably my first fully formed memory.

We lived in a traditional terraced house. Downstairs was the living room with the kitchen attached, upstairs had two bedrooms and the toilet was outside. If there was noise anywhere, you'd hear it. When I was woken up one night by shouting and flashing lights, it was only natural that I'd get out of my bed to have a nose. The racket was coming from Mum and Dad's room. As I stood at the door, I could see my gram standing at the side of the bed. Mum was holding the tiniest baby I'd ever seen and there was a doctor and ambulance men (as we called them back then) all fussing round.

'Get back to your room, Mandy!' shouted Gram, but I was mesmerised by it all and wasn't shifting, no matter what she said. Gram and Grandad only lived two doors down from us – and my great-auntie lived on the same road – so I can only assume that Dad had gone to get help and then this amazing thing happened. A baby had appeared! It was a miracle and I was just delighted that I'd been brave enough to get out of bed and wander through to see what was happening.

Mum and the tiny baby were whisked off in an ambulance as Gram ranted and raved about not being allowed in with them.

'That's my daughter! That's my granddaughter! I have every right to be with them – every right. How dare you! How dare you!' she went on. They weren't budging though and she had to huff and puff her way back in from the street, where a few of our neighbours were watching, having been woken by the flashing lights. Gram settled me back into bed but I don't have any other memory until sometime later, when I was taken into the hospital to see my new little sister.

I can't remember if it was Gram or Dad who took me, all I recall was a kindly nurse coming to greet us before we went into a little ward. I didn't know it was a special care unit, I wouldn't have had a clue about anything like that at such a tender age.

'Put these on, Mandy,' the nurse instructed me. She helped me with a mask and gloves, then took me into the room where the baby was.

'This is Fiona,' she said. The baby was in an incubator with tubes helping her to breathe, just a scrap of a thing, with me at the side of the plastic box trying to piece it all together. I'd certainly never been told Mum was pregnant and even if I'd noticed her tummy getting bigger, no one really spoke to kids about such things in those days. Now there was a sister.

I had just turned six when Fiona came into my life, but the biggest impact wouldn't come from a sibling being around but from the fact that her birth brought on postnatal depression in Mum. Of course, it wasn't diagnosed like that back then – if anything, people would say she had 'baby blues' – but it's clear from later medical notes that she suffered from that point on and that it would have a huge impact on her life, making her drink even more and causing her to be prescribed medication, usually Valium.

My memory jumps about so much – from Fiona being in bed with Mum when she was just born to visiting her in hospital, to being at junior school, which I'd only attended for a month or so before my sister came into the world. Apparently, I did go to nursery school as well but I've no recollection of that at all. The only way I know it happened is that I recently found a Facebook page where there were pictures of old schools I went to and I was shocked to find myself in some of them. I looked at a few and couldn't even recognise myself; if other people hadn't tagged the names to the faces, I wouldn't have had any idea. Even then, I found myself typing *Are you sure that's me?* to some of the comments. Other people have better memories of little Mandy than I do. There are pictures of me in a netball team and I honestly cannot remember ever playing netball in my life. I've not only blocked out memories of the abuse but also of my younger days. It's as if my mind is a circuit board where only certain parts light up and they'll never be brought to life again, the connections are completely gone and there's nothing to make it all work.

From what I can remember though, I did love school. It was my escape from what was a very unloving life to begin with, then from the absolute horror that was to come. I had friends, I could do what I wanted without getting shouted at, it was a hundred times better for me. I loved reading and would devour my gram's Catherine Cookson novels even though they were completely inappropriate! I think every young girl my age probably had those as her early readers – the tales of evil mill-owners and landed gentry doing what they wanted made up my bedtime reading more than Winnie-the-Pooh or Enid Blyton ever did! I certainly didn't have much else to keep myself occupied; the only toy I owned was a racing car set. I didn't have a doll or a pram or even a teddy bear.

I was looked after in the most basic ways – I was clean, fed, watered – but there was no compassion or love. The only warm moments came from Gram. From the day I started, I walked to school on my own, making sure that my first stop was at the pub where she cleaned. She'd give me a packet of crisps for my break, which I always ate on the way to school, and I'd go back to her at lunchtime for a sandwich. She worked incredibly hard, always had a few jobs on the go, and would tell me stories about the filth she'd found in the pub that day or the disgusting things people had left behind. I'd listen to it all with open ears and wide eyes, but all I really wanted was to be with her as it felt much cosier than at home. She didn't gush or cover me with kisses and tell me I was her Little Princess, but she did give me a calmness and security I never felt in my own house. When I was there, I only worried if Mum was going to be drunk and, increasingly, what Dad's reaction to her state would be. They shouted at each other constantly and he was always looking for something she had done wrong – or not done at all. He was confident and restrained in some ways, he never swore that much, but he was threatening and violent to her and I hated it – not because of overwhelming love for Mum (she certainly didn't encourage that), but because it was a toxic, unpredictable way for any child to live.

I had friends in school but none on the 'outside' as it were – when I was little, I only once had a sleepover and it was an eye-opener. The girl's parents were so lovely – they helped us put cushions in the middle of the room to jump on, they gave us snacks and seemed genuinely loving towards their little daughter – it was another world to me. I do think it only happened that once as Dad wasn't keen on me having contact with anyone else outside the house.

My world was tiny. The house we rented until I was about seven, the one with the outside loo, was really small and there was no room for any privacy. There is one strange memory I have from there which I just can't seem to make any sense of. One day, when I came back from school, I climbed up the stairs to the attic and it was full of books, like some sort of library. I got shouted at by Dad for that and never tried it again. I don't even know if that's a real memory or something that has been in my mind for such a long time that it seems real, but I think it genuinely happened. It raises a lot of questions though – what were the books? Who did they belong to? And why did no one ever speak about it?

We were given a new council house when I was about seven as ours was being pulled down. Gram and Grandad would still only be a couple of houses down again and I was really relieved about that. We'd have the glamour of an inside toilet too!

Gram was always in the background if we needed her. Mum and Dad never gave me a penny of pocket money, but Gram did. She also made sure that I never went without, buying me clothes and even getting her sister to make me dresses. My grandmother gave me everything as my parents just weren't bothered or so it seemed. If she was sorting me out, then they obviously didn't feel they had to. I suppose now I wonder how much of the household money Mum was spending on drink, but back then as long as I was getting what I needed from Gram, I was content just being with her – Gram was my stable influence.

As I grew older, she never became any more affectionate but she continued to show her love for me in lots of other ways. It's crazy to think she was probably younger than I am now, but grannies seemed like grannies back then. In fact, they were old ladies just by virtue of being a granny.

I think they were also pretty stoical and although Gram must have been frustrated at how useless my parents were, she just stepped up when she needed to.

Although I remember Gram as clear as day, I can quite genuinely say to you that I remember only a handful of moments from those initial times at school until I was 11. It's like my life didn't exist until I was 11, until the point where I can remember every single day. However, after Fiona was born, there were a few incidents which jog my memory. Mum and Dad started arguing even more. She was drinking a lot – always bingeing rather than starting early every morning and keeping going all day, every day – and when she did, the record player would go on. Roy Orbison would start warbling and the whole cycle of drink and melancholy would begin. She would drink herself into oblivion on those occasions and I'd often come in to find her collapsed on the sofa. Sometimes my parents went out together as Dad too was a drinker back then, and when they did, I was the babysitter.

I must have only been about seven when on one of those Friday nights, Fiona tripped over the rug while I was playing with her on the floor and started screaming.

'Oh God, oh God!' I shouted. 'What's wrong with you, what's wrong?'

She was getting more and more worked up, then blood began pouring from her mouth. I knew I had to get Gram, so I ran as fast as I could to her house, leaving Fiona screaming. I couldn't have carried her and I was far too little myself to really think anything through rather than get a grown-up.

Gram raced back with me, rushed over to Fiona and scooped her up.

'Go back and tell your grandad to get to the pub for this poor child's mother. It's a bloody disgrace that they've left you alone with her!'

I did as I was told. By the time I got back, Gram was rocking Fiona on her lap and all of the blood had gone.

'She'd only bitten her lip, Mandy. She'll be fine,' I was told.

I felt so guilty and by the time Mum and Dad came back, I knew that it was all going to kick off. Gram told them just what she thought of them but they both blamed me.

'Why didn't you look after her properly?' Mum shouted once we were all on our own. 'Why did you have to go running to her so she can tell me what a shit mother I am?'

There was nothing to say. I'd have been terrified to go to the pub for her, leaving my little sister bleeding – and anyway, she *was* a shit mother.

Dad was still working in a factory doing shift work at the time we moved into our new house but he left that job quite soon after to start up as a taxi driver for a local man who had a private hire company. It didn't keep him out of the house enough and they fought constantly.

I came in from school one day and it was like a war had broken out.

'You're a liar!' Mum was screaming. 'You're a liar, Keith Meadows, and I know you're seeing another woman!'

'You know nothing,' he replied, calmly. 'You're making it all up – as usual.'

'What's this then?' she shouted. She threw a box at him and he left it where it landed on the floor. 'You don't have to open it, do you? You don't have to because you know what's in there.'

He shrugged.

'What is it then? You tell me.'

'It's a necklace – it's a fucking necklace for HER! Your Australian fancy woman!' They didn't even notice that I was there as they went full pelt for each other. 'I know all about her! I know you met her through the taxis, I know you're planning to run away with her.'

'If you know it all, you don't need any answers from me then, do you?' said Dad, calmly. With that, he walked out of the room, leaving Mum wailing in anguish and swearing into thin air. Dad never swore though – it was another way in which he thought he was better than anyone else. That fight is certainly one memory etched in my mind even though so many others are missing.

Mum was right: Dad did have an Australian fancy woman and he was planning to leave us all for her, but somehow it petered out – from the other woman's side,

I'd guess. Sadly, we were stuck with him. Before that happened though, Mum left as a result of finding out about the affair and we all stayed with Gram for a while. For that short time, it was pretty calm and I loved living away from Dad.

The police seemed to be at our door a lot and I can piece together some of that now: it was all to do with Mum's behaviour. By then, we'd moved back in with Dad and had moved to another new house. My mum's mental health issues were getting worse – in fact, she would end up in psychiatric units as I got older. Over the years, I've collected corners of stories and tried to build them up into a picture of how her life was, but the gaps are huge. Gram told me that Mum had a few miscarriages, which makes sense given that there are at least five years between each of us girls. She also told me that she once found Mum bleeding in a phone box, calling for an ambulance. Gram also said that Dad had beaten his own father with a dog lead, with no context of why or where. These were all just snippets which were thrown at me, at the little girl who was lost with no comfort at home and no strong foundations of love, receiving snatches of adult lives and adult complexities which she couldn't even begin to understand.

Another strange thing was that my maternal granddad had a suitcase under his bed, which was filled with old newspaper clippings. It's all muddled up in my head, but I remember seeing that some of them were about Mum.

One of them I read said that she had been up in court for sending a wreath to someone who was very much alive and there were words thrown about like 'harassment' and 'restraining order'. These were patterns of behaviour from her that would deepen and develop – all of those words in the newspaper clippings didn't make much sense to me then but they certainly would in later years.

Things were changing a bit – and not for the better. When I was little, I'd just been pretty much ignored while Mum and Dad fought, but now the impact of her illness, their bitterness and the violence were all filtering through to me.

One day, when I got home from school, the front door was wide open.

I stepped inside and called out, 'Mum?' There was no reply but as I glanced around, I noticed drops of blood on the floor. I followed the trail all the way up the street to the house of a friend. Mum was there, crying, and when she left, I had to stay. I don't know where she went, I don't even know if the police took her, or if she went to hospital, but there was now more drama in our lives than there had been before.

On another occasion, when I got home after school, the police were inside and one of them told me not to come in. I just accepted that. Often there were windows boarded up. Maybe Mum was self-harming, maybe she was just angry about something – who knows? I don't even remember the outcomes of a lot of this stuff, it was just the background to my life.

There were more physical fights too. I came in one afternoon to find Dad had Mum pinned to the wall with a carpet sweeper. He was holding the long handle and prodding her with the main part of it, jabbing it into her stomach. All I could think of was to run to get my gram – we had no phone in those days – but, once more, it goes blank and I don't know how the story ends.

Dad had started to become involved with The Salvation Army once again – he'd repledged himself to God, which meant that I was dragged along too to make sure it looked as if he was extra-committed. I had to go to Salvation Army youth clubs and wear the uniform at Sunday School. I played the tambourine in the church meetings and was also in the Young Soldiers Choir. On Wednesdays and Thursdays, I had practice for both of them and on Sundays, I'd play tambourine or sing, whichever they decided they needed me for. I hated it all, but Dad clearly loved being in a uniform; I'm surprised he'd ever given it up in the first place. He enjoyed the status of any uniform all his life – he'd say that he liked the respect it gave him and it supported his notion that he was better than anyone else.

This was my childhood, this was my life. There was no warmth, no love unless it came from Gram. I'm not for one moment suggesting I was the only child ever to experience that, and it's certainly far too common even to this day, but what I do feel about my early life under those conditions was that it taught me just to accept, accept, accept. This was how things were. A girl like me didn't have the power to change, or even question, any of it. My parents didn't love each other, never mind love me, and Mum got through it all with alcohol, odd behaviour and shouting. Dad's approach was control. Always control. He was cold in a different way, a way that I would now see as sociopathic, a way that was to change my life forever. And did I ever think I could do something about it?

No.

Accept, accept, accept.

2

Such a Good Man

Indoors, Dad was just himself as most people are – I simply accepted who he was as I did with everything – but outdoors, in the world, he was someone else. He was full of self-importance when with his bowling club buddies, or with neighbours, and by the time he went back to The Salvation Army, he was glorying in that too. Dad had a lot of status in our community. He was an upstanding father, he was godly, he was sticking by his wife who wasn't 'all there'; he was a good guy. These men often are, aren't they?

I guess I've danced round him a bit so far and I probably need to force myself to go back. I don't really want to think of him at all, but in terms of how he looked, he was tall with quiffed mousy blond hair. He liked the latest fashions and always wore quite smart clothes. I guess that making sure he always looked presentable and smart was part of his act of seeming like an upstanding man. His music of choice was Jim Reeves which, to me, was just as miserable as the Roy Orbison songs that Mum was always blasting out. Mum was quiet if she was sober, but Dad was the boss no matter what, by far the dominant one in their marriage and someone who made sure she did what was expected of a good wife. As I've said, she had to clean, she had to keep a good house and if she didn't – whether through being drunk or him imposing some new standards out of the blue – then we'd all know about it.

Home was a place where I had to do what I was told to. I had to be in bed at a certain time – 6 p.m. when I was at this age (I would have been around 8 or 9 years old) even when it was light in summer. I'd lie in bed, listening to the other kids all laughing and playing outside, but I'd never have got up or asked to be allowed to stay up longer. I knew what was expected, I always did. My room had to be spotless and Dad would give me an absolute bollocking if there was anything out of place. I'd shove everything under my bed to keep it tidy, but he cottoned on to that quickly and I'd get short shrift: 'You're lazy, Mandy – you're a very lazy, messy little girl.'

There was no shouting, no screaming, just cold words and a look that made me think he saw me in the same category as Mum: someone to be kept under the thumb, someone to be watched and punished if needs be.

If I was abused before I was 11, if that's why I have so few memories, I don't want to know. What I do remember is bad enough, I don't want to add to it. Maybe it started in one of the other houses, maybe it had been going on for years. I have often wondered but I've never followed through; I've never looked at it in any more detail, partly for fear of what I might find in my own memory. Maybe I've put earlier stuff into a little box and only allowed my thoughts to go to what happened once I was 11. I'll never know, not without therapy I guess, and I'm pretty sure I don't want to. That doesn't stop it from being something which niggles at some points, but it is what it is. I know that I've dissociated from a lot of things, but I also know that I don't particularly want to go back and unpack it all, so I think of those years as ones in which he frightened me by his behaviour with Mum and by his way of treating me when, for example, I wasn't tidy enough for his liking.

By the time we'd moved to our second house, the fighting between Mum and Dad was getting worse. He used to spit at her and hit her with things; I'd come down in the morning to rooms that looked as if a bomb had gone off. The curtains would be ripped from their poles, cupboards emptied with the contents lying on the floor, glasses and plates smashed – I'd have been listening to it as it went on, but the sight of it in the morning before I went to school showed just how toxic their relationship was.

Just stop, just stop, I would think to myself as I lay in bed, but I knew it had to run its course – they both needed to get it out of their systems. In the morning, she'd have marks all over her, he'd have scratches on his face, but none of the neighbours ever called the police even though they must have heard everything. It was all contained in the house, I guess it would just be brushed off as a 'domestic'. There would be plenty of homes where that would be happening, but it doesn't make it right. Back then, people would turn a blind eye, a deaf ear, to what went on between husband and wife, with little thought about how the children in the middle of it all were feeling.

If it was really bad, I'd go and get my gram, but if it was the early hours of the morning, I just had to wait it out. I would sleep with my fingers in my ears. I never knew if one of them would be dead when I woke up in the morning. Again, I just got on with it, the uncertainty and the violence were something I had to let happen. I was a little girl – what could I do?

There's a sense that children in violent households develop – you wait and you watch, constantly looking out for signs that things are going to turn. You are sensitive to every glance your parents make towards each other, you listen out for changes in the tone of their voices. You wait. You just wait because you know it's coming again just like it did all the times before and even though there's nothing you can do to stop it, you still hold your breath and wonder who will be standing when it's all over. Did I think they had the capacity to kill each other? Yes, I probably did because there was an almost animal-like quality to their fighting and I'd seen the remnants of those fights on too many morning-afters to pretend to myself that it would always be OK. One day, it could all be very different indeed.

Mum became pregnant with my second sister, Gillian, in the midst of all this and she was born in 1977. This was just before I turned 11 and we had recently moved to our third house. I try to remember dates but a lot of it is fuzzy, so I go by markers of what I have in my mind's eye – what address were we at, how far away from us was Gram, who were our neighbours, was there a park nearby or did kids play out in the street? It's my way of finding some sort of order in the chaos of my memories.

I can remember Mum leaving the house one afternoon and Dad saying, 'Your mother's gone to have the new baby, she'll be back when it's all over.'

I knew a baby was coming that time – I was obviously older than I had been when Fiona arrived – so I noticed Mum's growing belly and there was also the pretty clear presence of a massive Silver Cross pram in the corner of the living room, waiting for the new member of our family. I was excited at the thought of another sibling and it looked like it was all finally happening.

'Will she be long?' I asked.

Sighing, Dad said, 'No one knows these things, Mandy – she'll be as long as it takes.'

'Is it another girl?' I persisted.

'No one knows anything. You'll find out when she comes back. She's having a baby, that should be enough for you – it's all you need to know.'

Men didn't go to hospital with their wives back then, so I was stuck with Dad. I went to my room and read until it was dark, then lay there for a bit, wondering about the baby. I didn't have any idea what happened when women gave birth – we'd had no sex education in school and I knew nothing about the human body. I'd heard it was painful but the thought of a lovely new baby brother or sister made it seem worthwhile – for me anyway!

That night, Dad announced gruffly, 'You've got another sister – she's called Gillian.' I waited for some more information, but there was nothing. Again, that wasn't unusual for back then: kids were just told stuff as and when they needed it, they weren't brought into every conversation and decision. It was still exciting though, more so than when Fiona had been born because I'd be able to cuddle this baby lots and take her in and out of her cot. Maybe I'd even be allowed to take her for walks by myself in her pram.

'You better have a bath,' my father told me in a very matter-of-fact way.

Off the kitchen, there was our bathroom with no lock

on the door. It was Sunday night, bath night – you only got one bath a week back then and I planned to lie there for a while, enjoying the hot water and wondering if baby Gillian might make Mum and Dad get on with each other a bit more. Surely a new daughter would make them happy?

I'd not long been in the bath when Dad walked in to use the toilet and looked at me.

'You've got me all wet, I'll have to take my clothes off now,' he said.

That was it, that was how it all began.

There was no preamble, no sense of him leading up to it, just 'You've got me all wet, I'll have to take my clothes off now.' I didn't even understand. How could he be wet? I was the one in the bath, he hadn't been near the water. And why in the world would my own dad take his clothes off in front of me?

I was lying in the bath at the opposite end from the taps as he started to undress. I didn't want to see, so I closed my eyes and hoped he was just going to dry himself off with a towel, although we had some of those in the kitchen and surely it would have been better to use one of them? He didn't seem to be getting a towel though, he didn't seem to be leaving the bathroom.

I opened my eyes ever so slightly and peered at him, horrified to see that he had his pants, trousers – all his clothes off – and stood there naked at the side of the bath. I quickly closed my eyes again.

Gruffly, he told me, 'You'll have to stand up. And open your eyes, don't be stupid.'

'What do you mean, "stand up"?' I asked. 'Stand up in the bath?'

He nodded.

'Why? Why would I do that?'

'You'll do that because I'm telling you to do that, that's why. Hurry up!'

With that, he got in the bath beside me. I scrabbled to get up as the water splashed about and tried to lean against the wall behind as I didn't want to be lying there beside him as he had a bath – surely that's what he was planning? What other reason could he have for getting undressed and getting in? But why would he get into a bath if he was complaining about being wet already? I didn't want to watch my own dad washing himself, I couldn't think of anything worse. Not at that point …

As soon as he was in, standing in front of me, I could see that his thing was hard.

'Have you ever seen an erection?' he asked. I shook my head – I hadn't even heard the word before. 'Well, I'll show you. This,' – he motioned his head down towards it – 'this is one.'

All of a sudden, his wet hands were all over my body and I couldn't really understand what he was doing. Why did he want to do this, why did he want to touch my moo (as I called my private parts) and everything else? It felt like it was going on forever, so I just closed my eyes again and tried to block it out. Then he stopped and I opened my eyes: he was doing something to himself. His hand was going up and down his private parts and he was getting really excited, then suddenly he groaned and stopped. I could see all of this white stuff on top of the bathwater and had no idea what it was. As soon as it was out of him, he rose from the bath and got out.

'Look what you've done,' he said, glancing down at his private parts.

I could see the difference: it wasn't hard anymore, it was floppy. I had no idea why it had been one way or the other. I had absolutely no understanding of any of this, I'd never learned about this at school, I'd never seen anything that would shed a light on what happened with bodies in any way at all. He left me in the bathroom and I carried on with my bath.

What did I think as I was in there? I know that I thought I wanted to get out quickly because of the white stuff that was floating about, but I also thought that I didn't want to go anywhere in the rest of the house where Dad might be in case he showed me the thing again. Would it keep going that hard way? Would he always want to get in the bath with me now? Would he touch my moo again? It was too much to think about but I did get washed as much as I could, dried myself and ran to my room. I don't know if I was hurting – maybe not as much as I would have been if he hadn't done those things in the water – but I did try to just blank it out.

I never questioned it though; I got on with the rest of the night, like I always did. He was my dad and that had been what he wanted to do, so I'd let him. On a Sunday night, we all watched *Songs of Praise* and *Stars on Sunday* with Harry Secombe and Jess Yates. It was a family tradition for a good Salvation Army man and his family, so that's what we did that night.

'Come and watch the telly, Mandy,' he called as I was putting my nightdress on. 'It's nearly starting, hurry up!' So I went through to the living room, sat beside him as usual and we sat like a pretend perfect father and daughter, watching religious programmes as if nothing had ever happened.

I thought it was just a one-off. At least I prayed it was. Dad didn't tell me to keep it a secret, but he didn't have to. I thought it must be my fault, so why would I tell anyone that I'd done something wrong? After all, it was me who'd got him wet – I'd probably get in trouble if I admitted that even if I couldn't work out what I'd done in the first place. Watching telly went on as if nothing else had ever happened.

'Best get to your bed,' he told me after the programmes ended. 'School tomorrow and your little sister might be here when you get home.'

That's how so many abusers work though, isn't it?

They do what they want then carry on as if everything's perfectly normal. You're left questioning yourself, wondering if it even happened, trying to figure out if you imagined it – but then the reality kicks in and you know that you would never, could never, have imagined such a thing. You remember the details – the hard 'thing', the white stuff floating on the bathwater – and you know. You know it was real, but because you can't face up to it, you push it away, away, away. And that becomes your coping mechanism, that becomes your life.

When I got myself ready for school the next morning, I just concentrated on hopefully seeing baby Gillian later that day and was delighted when that happened. I ran into the living room and could hear a little whimpering noise from the pram in the corner.

'Christ, don't wake her!' sighed Mum from the sofa. 'I'm in bloody agony and the last thing I need is her kicking off, thanks to you running around like an elephant.'

She was a tiny little thing wrapped up in a white shawl. I put my finger into her hand and she clasped onto it.

'Look, Mum!' I said excitedly. 'She likes me! She's holding my finger.'

'Ssssh! Shut UP!' was her reply. 'Why don't you go to your room? I need a rest.'

Mum and Dad weren't exactly in a baby bubble. Life just went on. They still weren't affectionate with each other and Gillian just slotted in. Gram seemed to do more than Mum whenever she had time between her jobs, but I was becoming aware that Dad wasn't happy when she was around.

About a week after Dad had touched me in the bath, he came into my room one night. I was fast asleep when I felt a weight on my bed: it was him. It must have been in the early hours of the morning when, without a word, he'd just climbed in bed beside me. Of course, I was startled that time as he hissed, 'Shush, be quiet!' I prepared myself for that horrible touching again, thinking I must have done something else wrong just like in the bath, but what happened next was something I couldn't understand or explain.

Lying beside me without his own pants on, he manoeuvred my nightdress up, took my knickers off and stuck something into me. At first, I didn't even know what it was and then I remembered the thing he had shown me the week before. *Was it that? Had he put the thing inside me?* He had, I just knew he had. No sooner did the thought enter my mind than I was hit with a searing pain. Flinching, I tried to get into a position where it was more bearable and now I think, *how appalling is that?* I was trying to get more comfortable so that he could do *that* without making a fuss?

He moved about a bit, back and up and down, up and down, up and down, doing what he had to do, then pulled my nightie back down and stood up. After fixing my sheet and his clothes, he simply said, 'Don't tell anybody' – and that was it. He left my room and I was abandoned, 11 years old, lying there, wondering what on earth had gone on. There was a thought in my mind when it was happening that if I didn't move, I'd be all right, but how could I be? How could an 11-year-old be raped by her own father, the pain searing through her, and possibly be all right?

Writing this, something popped into my head – *I didn't bleed. My father raped me when I was a child and I didn't bleed.* It made me think – I was so young that it's quite odd that there was no blood. Was that because I was already used to it? Was that why I was so accepting?

I know that I got up, went to the loo for some toilet paper and wiped the stuff off my moo and my legs. As I looked down at the tissue, a horrible stench came off it that I couldn't describe – I truly had no idea what this awful goo was that came out of my father or what it meant, I just had to get rid of it. It wasn't bath night so I didn't know when I could next get a proper wash and I was terrified that I would stink of it. Afterwards I ran back to my room, wondering if he would do it again – that night or another night. Everything was topsy-turvy, everything was on its head, and I didn't have the words to describe what had happened that night or the time in the bath. I was lost already – and I was accepting of it all.

Maybe this was just what Dad did now.

Dear Mandy

I want to grab you – I want to rush into my own story and take little Mandy into my arms, to get you away from your father, your mother, your home. I want to save you because then I can maybe save me. Looking back at all of this is hard, not just because I'm having to look at what the people who should have loved you did to you, but because I can't do anything about it. You're such a tiny girl, the one who was always small, who always looked younger than her years, who was so innocent, so vulnerable and you don't know that you'll get through it. It won't be easy, but you'll get there. I know that Mandy can't imagine becoming the woman she is today and that hurts. Your pain is invisible to everyone and there are years and years of it to come.

I feel that I'm speaking a language many survivors will recognise all too well when I talk to you in my head, little Mandy. Looking back, I see the child I was and it breaks my heart. I love my own children with every fibre of my being. I'd kill for them, I'd die for them – and the knowledge that no one, *no one*, felt even a tiny part of that for you, or any child going through abuse, is the most awful thing.

How did you survive? How did *I* survive? By blocking it out, by accepting it, just by thinking it was how life had to be. If only I could scoop you up and promise you it will get better – but even doing that would come from the knowledge that you have much, much more to get through.

Mandy, when you hear the footsteps coming to your room at night, when you feel the weight of *his* body in your bed, when you close your eyes as tight as you possibly can as he climbs on top of you, know that you'll get there.

There is hope.

Love is waiting.

A good life will come.

But for now, it's hard, it's so very hard, and I wish I could make it all stop for you.

For *us*.

3

Special Time

In all honesty, I think I went into survival mode very quickly. The dissociation, the memory loss I have, I do feel that it was all part of the almost-immediate reaction I had to Dad's abuse. He didn't ramp things up slowly, he touched me in the bath and then he raped me the next time. I've read other books where the abuser grooms his victim, where he begins by groping perhaps, then after a while moves on to intimate touching, then finally feels he can get away with raping the child. My dad wasn't like that; he was confident from the outset. I don't know why he decided to start that night he abused me in the bath, what the trigger was for him – was it that he knew for sure that Mum was out of the house, having a baby? There was no way she would be back and maybe that was more of a guarantee than he'd ever had before. Although she could be drunk or sleeping on other nights, perhaps he always worried that she might get up or come to her senses.

Or perhaps it had been happening for much longer than I remember. Maybe I'd been accepting things for longer than I know. I do have to consider that – writing this and realising I didn't bleed the 'first' time he penetrated me is part of that growing awareness – but I don't think I'll ever know for sure. All I can do is tell the truth. I'll never embellish or pretend I know more than I do, and because of that, I can categorically state that everything I recall from that first time in the bath is fact.

Even on 'normal' nights, once I was in bed, I had to stay in bed. I wasn't allowed to wander about or pop to the kitchen for a drink – bedtime meant 'stay-in-bed' time. The third time 'it' happened, I heard the footsteps coming. I hadn't been asleep and I wasn't dozing so I just heard him getting nearer to my room, to me. We didn't exactly have a huge house, but I could still tell when the steps were coming towards my room rather than going to his. The door opened, then closed behind him and all I could think was, *he's here – it's going to happen again. That thing he did last time, he wants to do it again.* There was no other reason to be there, it wasn't as if he was going to read me a story or have a lovely father-and-daughter chat. He didn't say a word, he just pushed my nightdress up, pulled my knickers down and did it, covering me up with a sheet as he left. It was about a week after the first time he had done it and I was just numb.

Again, I lay there in the puddle of what he'd left. By the morning, it had all dried on the bedsheets. I pulled them off the mattress and took them downstairs to the wash-basket, focusing on the practical side of what had happened. By then I regularly changed my own bedding, which meant it wouldn't have aroused Mum's suspicions and besides it was just one of my many chores. I went to school and gave it no thought at all. Not a single thought – how horrendous is that? I'm bewildered by it myself – how can a child have that done to her and just get on with her day? I guess I knew nothing but getting on with everything, I just put everything into little boxes. This was another one, labelled *The Things Dad Does to Me*. A box that wasn't to be opened, but a box that would be filled up beyond my darkest thoughts.

As time went on, Dad took much longer but to start with, he'd just have his erection, do 'that', cover me up and leave. My room wasn't far away from the others but he seemed to have no concern about anyone hearing him. Mum was in bed early with her sleeping tablets and practically comatose anyway, but would she have cared? Later, I realised it was unlikely, but that's another part of the story.

The next time it happened, he told me, 'This is our special time.' But it didn't feel special, it felt horrific. 'You don't tell anyone. What you need to remember, Mandy, is that if you tell anyone about this, about us having a nice time, you'll be taken into care. No one will believe you.'

I've often wondered what on earth leads up to a man doing that to his own daughter, or to any child? He couldn't have just woken up one day and thought, *oh, my daughter's attractive, so I'll do this tonight* – and believe you me, I did think it was my fault for attracting him. Something must have taken him to that point. What was it? Had he been watching me for years and got to a point where he'd managed to convince himself it was fine? Have I repressed memories and he'd been doing it for years? Did something just break through in my mind with the bath situation and allow me to remember it from that point on? There are so many unanswered questions – and I don't want to know what those answers are.

It's only since writing this book that I've even called it 'rape'. I always said that he 'had sex' with me, that seemed an appropriate phrase, but it really isn't – it minimises and it cloaks what is really being done. When I read about fathers raping their children, it always seems to be called 'an incestuous relationship' and I feel that also minimises what is happening or has happened, it makes it softer. If it's 'only' incest – a word that's really tame compared to rape – then I haven't felt I have the right to call it anything else. It's someone you know, it isn't a stranger jumping out at you and dragging you down a dark alley. It's your dad, at home, in your own bed – and the word 'incest' just makes it all less horrific, doesn't it? It makes it easier for other people to dismiss it and find it almost acceptable. But it *is* horrific – it doesn't matter where it happens or who does it, it's rape, simple as that. I only came to terms with that very, very recently. But, you know what? Calling it rape makes me feel even shittier – if that's possible – because it's something that you can't hide behind in any way, shape or form.

So, I might not have known Dad was raping me from when I was an 11-year-old child, but I damn well knew I hated it. As I said earlier, we'd had no sex education at school and we certainly never talked about that at home, and I was completely baffled by what he was doing – in fact, I didn't *know* what he was doing, but I just had to let it happen. I had no idea why he was sticking *that* in there and moving it about, but he told me it was what dads did, it was their way of showing affection, so that was that.

'This is how I love you, you're my special girl,' he'd say, 'but you're not allowed to tell anyone – it's our secret, you know that? This is what dads do with their daughters, people just don't talk about it. It shows I love you, but don't ever, ever tell anyone. They'll blame you, Mandy.'

He'd never, ever said I was special or that he loved me before that. You'd think I'd have been happy to hear it, however awful that sounds, but it just meant he'd created a huge conflict. You want your parents to love you and say you mean the world to them, but we'd never been an affectionate family; now I was getting that, but at a huge cost. I wanted the words, I wanted the affection, but I didn't want what he was doing to me – if this was the only way he could show me affection, then it must be normal, mustn't it?

I love you, Mandy.

You're special, Mandy.

Don't tell anyone.

No one will believe you.

You'll be taken away.

I'll go to jail.

You'll break up the family.

This is what dads do anyway.

This is because I love you so much.

You're special, special, special.

How could I fight any of that?

The more confident he got, the more it became a routine – three times a month at least without fail. On top of that, he was turning me into a little prisoner. Once he started raping me, almost immediately he kept me by his side whenever he could. If he went bowling, I had to go with him. If he went to the local shop, he took me too. If he went to work out of my school hours, I would be dragged along. He wouldn't let me out of his sight if it could be avoided. It all added to the conflict. He'd never taken me anywhere before and even though I didn't want to go to all these places, it was part of his control, part of his manipulation of me. Don't let me out of his sight, tell me I'm his special girl over and over.

Mum accepted it all, she never questioned why he was taking me everywhere all of a sudden. Did I want to tell her? No, because of the threats he made. Yes, because I wanted someone to save me. Even at eleven years old though, I wasn't daft enough to truly believe it would be her. She could barely live her own life, never mind save mine. On top of that, she had a small child and a baby to look after.

Dad continued to rape me at least three times a month. I'd got a telly for Christmas, and one night I was singing into my hairbrush, watching *Top of the Pops*. He came in and started doing all this stupid dancing, trying to make himself out to be friendly and nice. But it didn't fool me and it didn't take long before he sidled up to me with the usual words: 'I love you so much, Mandy – you're my best girl. We'll get married one day, you know.'

Now this was new. I was thinking, *what are you talking about? You're married to my mum. You're my dad, how in the world can I marry you? Why would I want to, even if we could? You disgust me, you absolutely disgust me.*

'Yeah, whatever,' was my only response.

'Come and sit on the bed with me, come and sit on the bed.'

'No, I don't want to!' I snapped back and went downstairs.

He followed me into the living room and just stared at

me. Mum was in bed by now – as usual, she went very early if she'd taken one of her tablets.

'Mandy, what are you doing?' he asked.

'Nothing.'

'I'll ask you again – what are you doing?'

I didn't look at him, I just answered, 'Nothing,' again. It did nothing but delay it a night and I knew when I was raped the following evening, there wasn't actually any point in refusing – I'd only be delaying the inevitable. It was an early lesson but quickly learned.

During the day when no one was in, or in the early evenings before I was in bed, I'd try to swerve it, but he always found new ways. He'd take me in the car with him and park up somewhere no one could see us. He'd start touching me all over, but there were times when I could get out and make my own way back home if we hadn't gone too far. His favourite place was a lake outside of Halifax. On the way there he'd buy me chips and as I ate them, he'd sit there with his hand on my leg and quickly work up to where he wanted to go. I got out of the car whenever I could but it was often only to, again, delay things because we were frequently in places where I would be stranded if I didn't get back in. I don't remember him ever raping me in the car, he just touched and touched and touched.

He'd be furious whether I left the car and walked home, or left the car and accepted that I had to get in again.

'Get back in that car now!' he'd snap.

'I don't want to.'

'Well, I'm telling you to – get back in right now!'

He'd drive back to ours like a lunatic in silence. Still, he never swore. During the day or those early evenings, I knew the touching was wrong, but when it was dark, I felt as if something had switched and he got to do whatever he wanted. When we were in the car, I felt as if I would be horrified if someone saw us, but at the same time, I wanted them to see and help me. Surely, they would know what he was doing wasn't right and put an end to it? I knew very early on that it was wrong, that I wanted to get away, but that I couldn't tell anyone as no one would believe me and I'd be taken into care. I wanted the decision made for me.

It was a routine – during the night, no foreplay (although that is such an awful word to use, I mean that he just penetrated me immediately), pushing into me until he was done. My gram used to buy me long nighties – really ugly, old-fashioned things – and quilted dressing gowns. I started wearing them in bed, even though I'd hated them before, because I thought *if I wear these, I'm not attractive – and he'll stop*. It made no difference at all – why would it to a man like that?

He'd just push them aside, he wouldn't have cared what they were.

'Mandy, I love you,' he'd grunt at me. 'This is how I show you I love you, this is what loving dads do. We'll be together soon, Mandy, we can run off soon. You'll be my wife, Mandy, we'll be a real couple.' He was like a broken record and yet, despite all those claims that he loved me so much, he never mentioned such adoration other than when he was raping me. The other Dad still looked out in case I wasn't tidying my room properly or minding my sisters. He still expected me to make cups of tea and help keep the house in order. The love he professed was only within the confines of that bedroom and the abuse he inflicted on me when he was there.

When he tried to touch me during the day, Mum would either be at Gram's or I'd be upstairs, where he had free rein. If she did go out, he'd say, 'Just leave her with me.' He would often cover it with other things – for example, we had an apple tree in the back garden and he wanted a vegetable patch, which meant he'd claim to Mum that I'd be helping him with those. But he'd always try to touch me. Always. I remember him taking me to a Cliff Richard concert once – who I hated anyway – and he tried to touch me in the car, but I managed to stop him. I think that, as I've said, that was all about building up a 'special' relationship. I was getting attention from him that my sisters never got, but it came at a price.

The most awful price.

It should have been normal, these were things you just do with your dad – trips out and the like – but they weren't things I'd ever done before and it confused me. Why was he raping me, why was he doing these awful things at night when he could choose to be a dad who took me places and did nice things at other times? Why did he mess up those nice times by often trying to abuse me when we were going places or coming back from them? My head was a mess and the only way I could cope was to – as usual – zone out and accept everything.

It felt as if it was only really ever him and me; he was isolating me very quickly. I never had any friends come to the house and I rarely went anywhere other than to my grandparents. There was no one to confide in if I did find the strength, no teachers or parents of friends, and I was terrified of the threats he repeated anyway.

Dad had applied to become a prison warden but he failed the maths exams, so decided he'd apply to join the Special Constables instead. This was the volunteer section of the police force and every area had them, but he built it up into something much bigger than it was. He was successful in his application and absolutely delighted that he had a uniform, handcuffs and a truncheon to boot. That made him even scarier – in my eyes, he *was* in the police. Dad had always told me that if I disclosed the abuse to anyone, I'd be in trouble – now he was one of the people who could throw me into jail.

He'd come home and say he'd been out looking for The Yorkshire Ripper, but it was all nonsense – he only did weekend evenings and usually it was just security guard-level stuff at concerts and things like that. The only difference between his uniform and that of the real police though was that his had the letters 'SC' on it: who would bother to look at that? They just saw the man who was always dressed smartly, with his shiny shoes and neat demeanour, fitting in time for community duties even when he had so much else to deal with at home. People worshipped the ground he walked on. Keith Meadows was the man who looked after his wife with all the mental health problems. She got sectioned, she drank, but he stood by her and made sure the family had a roof over their heads and food on the table. He was in The Salvation Army and now he was a special constable too. What a great guy he was, providing for us all. How could I ever say anything about a man with such a reputation? An 11-year-old girl claiming that he – her own dad – was raping her? Who would believe such a thing, who wouldn't think that it was the girl who was an evil liar?

The abuse had turned into something so regular that it was almost no surprise to me when it happened. He seemed untouchable, whether it was at home or out and about, and I had no reason to believe that anything was going to change.

It wasn't long after the abuse began that I had my first period.

Mum never warned me what was coming, so on the night that I went to the loo and found myself covered in blood, I was clueless. I went back into the living room and shouted, 'I'm dying! Help me, I'm dying!'

'What the hell are you going on about?' Mum said, as usual half-comatose from all her medication.

'I'm covered in blood!'

She peered at me. 'I can't see anything.'

'No, that's because it's in my knickers – it's coming from … down below. It's coming from my moo!' I was mortified at having to say it out loud because Dad was sitting on the settee, quietly taking it all in. Just watching, just listening.

'Oh, for God's sake, Mandy!' exclaimed Mum. 'You're not bloody dying!'

'It's just what happens,' Dad said. 'It's a period. You'll get that every month. It means you're a woman now, Mandy. Get her some stuff, Jenny. Get her sorted.'

Sighing, my mum dragged herself off the settee and went for some pads, which she threw at me as if she couldn't be bothered with any of it, settling back down into the sofa and continuing to watch telly.

I was horrified. I worked out that these pad things needed to go in my knickers and that they would soon be soaked in blood. I'd swap one for another, but that first night, I did think there was something horrifically wrong with me; no one had actually told me what a 'period' was, just that it meant I was a woman.

I got some answers from girls at school the following day but none of it was comforting. This was going to happen again! This was going to happen not for months or years, but for decades! How did the world go on with this sort of thing happening to women all over the place? There could be women and girls walking past me, bleeding, and everything went on as normal. Why had no one told me and what in the world was I going to do when it kept appearing every single month?

The next time it happened, I was still appalled but thought, *oh, Dad was right – it's come again.* Those words of his still ring in my ears: 'You're a woman now, Mandy.' I wasn't, I was just a little kid – but that didn't matter to him. I guess in his eyes, I *was* a woman given that he was making me do the things an adult would do and now my body was agreeing too.

I'd not been having my monthly bleeds long when Dad suddenly announced, 'Now you're a woman, you need to go on the Pill. It'll make your period less heavy, it'll help you.'

I wasn't part of the discussion – as always, I was just told what to do. Mum told me the next day that we were going to the doctor and when we got there, she told him, 'She's started her period and it's really heavy. She can't cope with pain, she's useless – she needs to go on the Pill.'

I'd only just started, I had no idea whether my periods were heavy or not, but I could certainly cope with pain, given what my dad was doing to me. They had colluded on that, it seems obvious now. He must have gone to Mum and said, 'Get Mandy on the Pill.' And she must have thought ... what? What could she have thought? *Oh, that sounds normal – my husband has just told me to get my 11-year-old daughter on the Pill. I won't question that at all, I'll just get it done.* It's incredible isn't it? And the GP just accepted it. What was he thinking too? All of them just deciding a little girl would be given contraception and it falling into place for *him*.

This is what makes me laugh when paedophiles say they just can't help themselves, that it's a disease, that it's something they don't choose. They're liars, every last one of them. My dad *chose* to rape me and then when I got my period, he *chose* to get Mum to agree to put me on the Pill. If he couldn't have helped himself, how come he only did it in my room when she was off her face? If it was something he had no control over, why wasn't he doing it to me in the street, in the living room when everyone else was there, in the chip shop when we stopped off before one of the drives? Isn't it just ever so convenient that this condition, this terrible affliction paedophiles have, only tends to reach fever pitch in secret?

And then *it just so happened* that my dad didn't come out and say to Mum, 'Here, Jenny, I'm raping our daughter pretty often now, so best get her on the Pill now that she's started her periods.'

They're not just liars, they're clever liars. If they put all that energy and brainwork they use up on abusing babies and kids, into doing something good, the world would change overnight. Instead, my father decided that, as the good man he and our community knew he was, it would be much better to keep it all quiet.

For me, for the 11-year-old me this was happening to, it was a thing of shame and terror, but for him, it was something nice. He was ramping up telling me that he loved me, that we were going to run away together, that we'd get married, and it never seemed to occur to him that all the times I tried to escape from the car or do anything I could to avoid my body being near his when we were in the same room meant that I hated every fibre of his being.

I wish I could talk to her – I wish I could go back to that little Mandy and tell her that she has nothing to be ashamed of and I wish I could tell her that she'll survive, that it will get darker, that it will get worse – oh so much worse – but that she is strong, she is a fighter, and she must hold on to that hope that one day she will be loved, one day she will know what a normal life is, but for now … For now, I'm so afraid for that lonely little girl with the parents from hell and not a glimmer of light in her world.

4

Don't You Believe Me?

We were in House Three for four years from when I was 10 and we moved out when I was about 14. The thing is, even in the midst of abuse, life goes on and for me, other things happened even when the constant rapes were the background to my world. One of my strongest memories from then, apart from my dad, was having my first love. I met Jake on the rec – the recreation ground – in the local park. I had just turned 13 when we started chatting on one of the few times I was allowed out. It was rare for me to be there, but I guess Dad also knew that he had me under his thumb – if I was going to run away, I'd have done it by now.

Jake was known as a bad boy locally: he'd been in borstal and was known for drinking and thieving, and that was what I was attracted to. He was actually four years older than me, which is horrific to think of now, but he never pushed me into anything – no doubt because he was seeing so many other girls and doing things with them. For us, all we did was sit together at the rec and hold hands, or creep into his house when his mum was at work. We truly didn't even kiss, we just watched telly, chatted, picked local heather and ate cheese and onion crisps! Being with Jake made me quite cool among the other girls. Everybody fancied him but he was mine – at 13! I think he was probably seeing half of the other girls around our place and definitely going further; I was just someone to be mates with but it still gave me some status.

I did get little bits of happiness when I was with Jake as he was a lovely lad to me but I should have known it wouldn't last. If Dad was still working after school, I'd meet Jake at the rec or have those 'watching telly' moments at his house, but I should have known my dad would find out.

I came back one day to find him waiting on me, sitting on the sofa when I had thought he would still be at work.

'Where have you been?' he asked.

'School.'

'It's a bit late to be claiming you've just come from school, Mandy, isn't it?'

I'd stopped off at the park to see Jake but hadn't really been there for too long.

'Well, it's true.'

'Don't you dare talk back to me like that! You've been with a boy, haven't you?'

I shook my head.

'You have, you've been with a boy and you're a little slag – admit it!'

'I haven't.'

'Mandy, I saw you. Stop lying, stop being a lying little slag!'

If he'd seen me, he must have been looking for me. Had he watched me leave school, followed me and then saw us meet up? There was nothing bad for Dad to see if that was what had happened, but for him, anything was bad that he hadn't expressly allowed.

'Well, you'll never see him again,' I was told.

'See who?'

'Don't you dare. Don't you DARE!' he snapped as his hand slapped against the side of my bed. 'If you see him again, if you go near him again, you'll wish you'd never been born! Do you understand?'

I was pretty close to wishing I had never been born anyway, but I nodded and any time I saw Jake after that, I would just walk past him, head down, silent. I don't suppose he would have been bothered, there were plenty of girls who gave him a lot more than I did, but it upset me more than anything else going on in my life at that time because Jake had been a little bit of happiness that I thought Dad couldn't touch.

Dad had moved on to abusing me at least every week and his confidence must have been through the roof as I still hadn't told anyone. I never moved on from just 'getting on with it', but by this time, I had also developed another way of coping; if he was doing it to me, he wasn't doing it to my sisters and that thought gave me some comfort. If I stopped him – although God knows how I would do that – I was terrified he would just move on to one of them. I didn't want Fiona and Gillian to ever go through what I was going through; I had to protect them, although I'll never know if I managed. I just know that I didn't care what happened to me as long as they were safe.

There's a big difference between a 10-year-old and a 14-year-old but one thing that didn't change in that house was him. Even without the sexual abuse, he was a horrible man. Whatever he said, went – he made the rules and I had to jump. Dad was also very good at picking up on any weaknesses, making sure to control me even more through them. For some reason, I had become terrified of fire and matches. We had a gas oven and I just couldn't light it, no matter what – I just couldn't hold that match to the gas and see the flame spark into life. He would taunt me mercilessly about that.

'Are you scared you'll go on fire, Mandy? Scared you'll go up in smoke? Well, we all will one day. Go on, try it, don't be so pathetic!'

I kept well away but he taunted me constantly. I remember one day sitting round the kitchen table with him, Mum and another woman. I always had to be where Dad was, he made sure of that and this day was no different. Mum used to collect money from neighbours who did the football pools. She gathered it all up, sent their slips away and deposited the cash at the Post Office. The other woman had called round to pay her money and the three of them were casually chatting while my mind was wandering. All of a sudden, I mentally came back into the room when I heard her complimenting Dad, who had walked over to the oven and started making the spam fritters he loved.

'Look at you, cooking for them all as well!' she gushed. 'I don't know how Jenny and the girls would cope without you, Keith – you're a hero to this family, you really are.'

Dad was glowing at her words but something snapped in me and I said, 'I hate him – I wish he was dead.'

'Do you now? Do you, Mandy?' he calmly questioned as the woman looked on in horror. She and Mum just sat there in stunned silence.

'Mandy, get over here,' Dad demanded with a face like fury.

'I'm not coming,' I replied. 'I don't like coming anywhere near that cooker, you know that.'

His face darkened. 'I told you to get over here and that's exactly what you'll do,' he snapped.

I walked over cautiously, knowing that I couldn't stand my ground – he'd make things even worse if I did. He grabbed my hand and held it over the flame.

'Stop it, Dad! I hate it!'

He dropped my hand closer and closer to the flame and, as the heat intensified, I could feel panic rising. Finally, I felt the heat on my skin and managed to pull my hand away. He smirked as I did so, knowing that he'd won again. It was all about control and this time, he was happy to do it in front of other people, even an outsider. I've got a scar to this day, a physical one to match the emotional and psychological damage he's done – and it wouldn't be the last. Mum carried on counting the pools money and when it was over, the other woman tutted and I knew it was at me, not him.

Someone else who won't save me, I thought.

Throughout those years I read anything I could get my hands on. I loved biographies and grabbed any books that were given to other people for birthdays or Christmas – I just wanted away from my own reality and escaped to my bedroom as soon as I could. It was my only outlet really apart from seeing my friend Hazel, whose mum was a mad Elvis fan. On a Saturday morning, we'd sit with her watching her video collection and that was lovely. Hazel's parents were so nice – her dad had pigeons that we visited and they all just seemed like a proper family. Dad was still allowing me to have a bit of contact with other people, but only on his terms, and he knew Hazel's family as her mum worked in a local shop he went to. Their life was another world, something I could only dream of – I knew it wouldn't just take a different dad to live that way, but a different mum too.

I was 14 when we moved to House Four. We'd always lived in council houses in the past, but Dad had a new job that came with accommodation this time. Predictably enough, it was a role that gave him a bit of status and power. He was now a caretaker in an all-girls' school and while that maybe didn't seem much more than a glorified janitor, it added to the idea in the community that Keith was to be trusted, he was someone you could rely on. After all, if even a school took him on to be in charge of all the maintenance, the gardeners and the cleaners, the responsibility of making sure that this posh school relied on him, well – he was just a good guy, wasn't he?

We moved away from the place where I'd been near my gram and friends, and now we had a two-bedroom bungalow for all five of us. It was a damp, dated place and I don't recall Mum ever decorating or trying to make it a bit homely. We never had modern stuff, it was always a bit old-fashioned, whether furniture or furnishings. There was a big family TV that you had to put 50p in to make it work and eventually a video recorder that was the only thing at all that made it feel we were finally in the 1980s.

The biggest issue for me once my dad was in that job

was that he could make sure I was by his side as much as possible. I couldn't pop in to my grandparents', I couldn't go out onto the street for a bit with mates, I was at his beck and call. As soon as he got the job, he told me that I'd be joining the cleaning crew morning and night, before and after school, which meant that he could even watch over me while he was at work.

Dad had left the Specials by then but was still going to Salvation Army services, although he didn't wear the uniform. We all had to go but didn't have to wear the uniform either. He loved having any power at all and soon became someone everyone working at the school could have a laugh with. The crew of women who cleaned every morning and evening thought he was wonderful and they probably just assumed he was a good dad, giving me the chance to earn a bit of pocket money. He would tell everyone else what to do, what to fix, where to clean, what bits of the grounds needed attention – he didn't do that much himself from what I could see; he was happier telling everyone else what their jobs were.

To begin with, my little sisters and I all shared one of the bedrooms but when Fiona was diagnosed with epilepsy and started having bad fits, it was an excuse to get them out of my room so that he could move in. A single bed was moved into our parents' room so that Gillian slept there, while Fiona was in the bed with Mum to make sure she was OK. To be honest, I don't see what Mum could have done because by that time, she was getting sectioned a lot and was drinking constantly. There were bottles of vodka hidden everywhere – her favourite place for the empties was in the spin dryer. When Mum wasn't drinking, she was crashed out from all the medication she was taking for her mental health problems. Having Fiona in her room for 'safekeeping' didn't make any sense at all as she wasn't sufficiently aware to be looking out for her, but it allowed Dad to do what he wanted to do, which was to openly, officially move into a bedroom with me: him on a single bed right next to mine.

He was still claiming we were a couple, still promising we'd run away together – and still saying that I had to keep quiet. 'People would think you were mad, Mandy – just like your mother. Don't you believe me? Don't you believe they would take you away and lock you up? You don't want to risk that, surely? Just stay quiet – we'll be able to leave together soon.'

I was isolated as much as possible. I wasn't living a few doors down from Gram and besides, over the past few years she had transferred a lot of her affection to my cousin, who lived with my grandparents alongside my aunt. I had still been visiting, but the sleepovers had long stopped. Now that there was more of a physical distance between us too, my contact with Gram dwindled. Dad hated me taking any time coming back from school as that would have been an opportunity to talk and build deeper friendships, possibly even go to my grandparents more – and who knew what might come of that? Maybe he thought I would tell, maybe he thought I would start asking questions or revealing things to the other girls, so he kept me on as tight a leash as possible.

If I wasn't at school, I was with him. When Mum was sectioned, I took over everything at home – to tell the truth, a lot of the time she was there, I did anyway as she was incapable of doing anything. He saw me as his wife in the house and the bedroom. I'd get up, give my sisters breakfast and see them to school and nursery. Then I'd go to my cleaning job at Dad's work before heading off to school myself. After school, I'd go to work and then do the housework and feed Fiona and Gillian when I got back. Then, when I should have been able to finally get some rest, he'd be there in my bedroom all night, falling asleep right beside me as soon as he'd finished raping me. He had free access to me all night and in full view of my mother. In fact, I wouldn't have been surprised if, even if he'd told anyone else he slept in the same bedroom as his daughter, they'd probably just see it as more evidence of what a great guy he was, a committed father.

Everything was about control. If I wanted to spend the money I was making, he had to come with me. He'd drop me off and wait for me, or on the rare occasions when I was allowed to meet friends, it would be for an hour at the shopping centre. We might go to a café, we might have a look around the record shops, look at the latest fashions in Tammy Girl, but Dad would always be in the car and I knew the clock was ticking. Being with friends was my only normal time, my only chance to be an ordinary teenager. Any time I bought a record or some jeans, there was a flash of *this is what other girls do*, but then I'd see him in the car, just waiting when the hour was up, and I was back into that world. I guess there was even the threat of my father when I had those little moments shopping because I'd never buy anything that 'showed off' my body, only ever jeans, terrified that I was doing something to make him abuse me, always ashamed that it was my fault and I made him unable to control himself. I wasn't allowed to wear anything revealing anyway but I would never have chosen to because of that fear.

I remember once just getting a dab of eyeshadow and mascara from a friend as we sat in a café. When he picked me up after an hour, he went ballistic.

'You look like a trollop!' he shouted at me. 'You'll get that washed off as soon as we get in.'

I knew he'd be like that; I'd just wanted to try it the once to feel normal. A few other times I experimented with make-up but washed it off before he collected me and soon gave up as it wasn't worth it. I got these snatches of being the girl I could have been – buying a record, looking at clothes, trying on a bit of make-up – but it was only for those single hours at a time before I went straight back to him.

I'd started smoking by then, a combination of having money from cleaning but also the usual peer pressure as everyone around me was doing it and also one of the few rebellious acts I could do, hopefully without Dad finding out. One day, he was going through my clothes, as he often did, and found a packet of cigarettes in the pocket.

'Whose are these?' he asked.

'My mate's.'

'Your mate's? You sure about that?'

'Yeah, yeah, I am,' I replied confidently.

The next day he did it again and I was daft enough to still have a few in my pocket.

'They're yours, aren't they?' he persisted.

'No, I've told you, they're my mate's. I promise you.'

He walked over to me with the cigarettes in his hand, broke them all up then scrunched them in my face, pushing the remnants in as hard as he could. But it didn't stop me.

It wasn't the only time. On one occasion, he'd gone to parents' evening – back then, kids didn't go, it was seen as something just for the grown-ups – and the deputy head dropped me in it. He'd caught me red-handed smoking behind the prefabs and saved it up until he knew that he was seeing my dad that night.

When Dad came home, I knew straight away because he had a lit cigarette in his hand – but he didn't smoke anything other than a pipe. I was sitting on the couch when he came up to me and said, 'You can't lie now.'

'What do you mean?'

'Mr Reynolds saw you smoking.'

I couldn't really go up against a teacher, so I said, 'Yeah, I was. Sorry.'

He got closer to my face and staring at me, he took hold of my arm, twisted it round and sneered, 'This is what happens when you get caught smoking. I've told you before and you didn't listen, did you? Well, maybe you will now.' With that, he ground the cigarette into my arm just above my wrist, looking into my eyes the whole time. I've got the scar to this day. As always, I refused to cry – even when he walked off, all I could think was, *But Mum smokes.* It wasn't really about that though, was it? It was all about power and control, just as it always was.

Boyfriends were the main issue. I was at that age when it would have been perfectly normal to start being inquisitive and to look for a lad to spend time with – a new version of Jake at the rec from when I was younger – but Dad made it clear that there would be hell to pay if that ever happened. The only way I would ever even be in contact with a boy would be at school or if it was someone through a friend, like their brother. I'd certainly started having more contact with other girls, getting a few friends as I got older, sometimes going to the shopping centre or just for a coffee as we all pretended to be older and more sophisticated than we were, but I had no interest in boys really – my experience of males was entirely through my dad and he wasn't exactly a glowing example.

It was just a life of him keeping me firmly under his thumb. Every day was the same. Mum's drinking was really bad, the sectioning was happening a lot, and I wasn't allowed to go anywhere unless he'd cleared it or was in charge of my comings and goings. He also had a pattern by now, which had ramped up since the early days of the abuse.

Monday, Wednesday, Friday and Sunday were rape nights.

I thought it couldn't get worse – I should have known better.

5

Family Time

Mum was usually in bed really early due to her meds. As soon as she went – and on those nights when he was set to abuse me – Dad would go for a bath. Afterwards he'd waltz into the living room just in his underpants, bold as brass, like he was God's gift. He'd park himself down on the settee as if he was King of the Castle. He always wanted me to sit in his lap and was really insistent one night.

'Come here, Mandy – come and sit beside me.'

'No, you're all right,' I told him, planning to get out of the room as soon as possible. It was a weekday night and I knew what was coming to me later but I didn't want to be near him for any other length of time.

'Come here – do as you're told,' he snapped. It was that tone of voice that I knew wasn't to be messed with and I didn't want a slap or a punch to come my way, so I went over.

'Let's watch a film,' he said. Not long before, we'd got a video player and he'd already put a tape in. There was no suggestion of what it would be and nothing could have prepared me. I thought it would just be a blockbuster film from the local video shop, but this was no ordinary film, it was something that I didn't even know the word for back then – but I do now.

Bestiality.

I couldn't even process what I was seeing. It was all taking place on a farmyard and there were animals doing things to women, men doing things to animals. The noises still haunt me – the screaming of the women, the squealing of the animals. It was the most disgusting thing I had ever seen.

I tried to get up, but he pulled me back.

'Sit on my knee, Mandy, sit on my knee! Let's have a bit of time together.'

'No! I don't want to watch that!'

'It's not a bad film, Mandy,' he tried to reassure me, 'just sit on my knee and watch it.'

I knew that I couldn't defy him constantly as I'd get my head butted, which had started to be one of his other favourite things to do to me, but there were a few occasions when it was almost as if the dam broke, as if the words were out of my mouth before I could stop them. I hated the consequences but I also wished that I could do it more, that I could stand up for myself. This time though, this time it was useless to say no as he was determined to make me watch these things. It was the beginning of him showing me bestiality videos regularly, probably once or twice a month. While he was raping me four times a week, the videos almost seemed like a 'treat' for him. He'd start moving his hand up my leg, stroking me, before getting to my private parts. He'd play with me there, on what I still called my 'moo', and I'd feel him getting aroused. Once the film was over, he'd snap, 'Bed now.' I'd dutifully go upstairs, he'd follow me, then he'd rape me with all of that still in his mind.

Afterwards, he'd get into his single bed next to my single bed in my room. I'd lie there staring at the stars on my curtains as he snored away contentedly. I still wasn't allowed to go to the toilet afterwards, I had to keep the smell of it on me.

The screenings moved on to lesbian pornography, couples or threesomes at times, never just men together, but it was the bestiality that really affected me. I'd keep my eyes on the bottom of the screen where it counted down how much time was left (always over two hours), but nothing could stop me from hearing what was happening. I had nightmares about dogs, cows, pigs, horses and from what I'd seen of those animals penetrating women and men penetrating animals too. I can only assume it was an under-the-counter video from the local shop and that he got all of his 'special' ones there. Who knows how he found out that they stocked them or how much of a market there was locally. I shudder even thinking of it. It was sick and I always knew that if he was sitting there in his underpants, he'd want me to be sitting on his lap and then the films would start.

I've read about it since and there are links between bestiality and child abuse. It should be a red flag, it should alert people. It was only when I read that material that I remembered other things about how Dad was with animals, with my pets – abusers often allow you to get emotionally attached to animals and then get rid of them or torture them. In House Three, I'd had two rabbits who bred and I was so excited when they had babies. Then I got up one morning and they were gone.

'Where are the rabbits?' I asked Dad.

'They're in the hutch,' he replied, off-hand.

'No, not the big one, the babies – where are they?'

He shrugged. 'Must have escaped.'

But I knew they hadn't – they were just little things, they could barely move. I was still upset as I walked to school that morning, the usual route I always took – the one Dad knew that I took. Under a privet, there was a pile of newspaper that had been ripped apart at one edge: I don't know if it would have been by an animal or a person. Inside were all my little bunny rabbits, all the babies – six or seven of them, all dead. I knew it was him, he'd taken them and just dumped them. And it didn't take him long to move on to the other two, the bigger rabbits.

I came in one day to Gram screaming at him, 'Why did you do that, Keith? You know she loves them!'

'What's happened? What are you talking about, Gram?' I asked.

'He's let your bloody rabbits go!' she replied furiously. 'He's taken them to the bloody golf course and set them off!'

'Did you, Dad? Did you?'

He shrugged the way he always did, a smirk on his face to show that he was enjoying it all. 'They'll be fine – they're rabbits, they should be in the wild.'

'Not pet ones!' shouted Gram. 'They won't last a bloody minute, Keith, and you know that. Imagine doing that to those poor innocent little things, knowing it would break Mandy's heart.'

But knowing it would break my heart was exactly why he did those things and both he and I were well aware of the fact. Raping me was the norm – actually, it was mine too. It was established, it was routine; I now feel that he pretty much used me as he would a prostitute. He never kissed me, never said anything while he was doing it, he just started and finished whenever he wanted. There was even one occasion when I woke up in the morning to find that he'd gone to work early and left money on my bedside cabinet.

Is that it now? I wondered. *Am I a prostitute?*

Whether it was a night I'd been raped, or a night when he'd made me watch pornographic videos as well, the next day was 'normal'. He'd get up and go to work, I'd leave at 7 a.m. to clean, then I'd go to my own school. I was actually doing OK at school simply because I've always compartmentalised everything. That was just how my life was. I couldn't get out of it, which meant I simply had to grin and bear it when it was happening and lock it away when it wasn't. There was me and there was *her*. During the day, I was me and on the nights he did that to me, I was *her*, I was *his*.

There was another continuing reason which helped me cope. As I've said before, while he was doing it to me, he wasn't doing it to my little sisters as far as I could see. Maybe that was what Mum felt too, maybe she was just grateful if he was keeping away from her. I never saw them being affectionate towards each other at all, but in retrospect, their fighting had definitely calmed down since he began abusing me. Perhaps she thought the same as I did about Gillian and Fiona – perhaps she was relieved he was abusing me.

I used to fantasise that he would get run over or drop dead of a heart attack. When he went jogging, I'd pray there would be a knock at the door.

'I'm so sorry,' the stranger would say. 'I've just found your dad stone-cold dead on the street. There's no way he'll ever be brought back to life. He's completely, definitely, absolutely dead – forever!'

If that wasn't going to happen, maybe I could hurry things along myself? Mum never let her medication out of her sight or I'd have been slipping Valium into his coffee, but there was one option I tried. She had loads of house plants and little bottles of Baby Bio everywhere, plant food to make them grow faster. I'd slip drops of it into his hot drinks and keep a close eye on him, hoping for immediate death. Actually, hoping for lingering, agonising death. But a couple of dribbles of off-the-shelf plant food didn't do the trick. I was stuck with him – I was also stuck with a life in which I was genuinely hoping I could do something to kill my dad. There might not have been any real attempt to do so, but if I could have been given the means, I would have grabbed it with both hands.

This was what life had brought me to, this was my reality.

He trained for half-marathons but I think even that had a sinister side. While out jogging, he could keep an eye on me. If I'd managed to get out for even half an hour, to sit in the park with friends and have a natter, he'd find me. He 'just happened' to be running past and he 'just happened' to see me in a group with a couple of boys in it.

And then he'd 'just happen' to batter me when I got home.

I only ever ran away once, to my friend's house in West

Layton, North Yorkshire, but her mum phoned him. I don't think I ever thought it would work, just like I didn't think there was any point in telling someone what was going on, and the fact that it failed simply reinforced that for me. My friends all had perfect lives with perfect parents, so I pretended I had that too. The only incident that ever happened to make me think others were maybe going through things was when a new girl appeared at school one day, out of nowhere, with no warning. She told us she was in foster care, but she didn't stay long, she disappeared as quickly as she'd came. Then we all saw the newspaper story about her which said her father had abused her and she was starting a new life. I thought, *how brave; I wish I could do that*, but who could I tell? Who would believe me? Dad was such a good guy, who would ever believe me over him?

By the time I was 15, I was still quite distanced from Gram too, which meant she wasn't an option as a safe haven or a confessional. I was constantly busy with cleaning and school, while it felt as though she had a new life now. Maybe I would have confided in her if things were different, but my father managed to isolate me from everyone, including my beloved grandmother.

One afternoon after school, Dad was out looking for me and he spotted me cuddling a boy in the park. In turn, I saw him coming towards me and ran as fast as I could to a friend's house. I went in the front door straight through

to the back door, coming out of that as if I'd been there all
the time. But he was waiting for me; he knew exactly what
I was going to do as if he could predict my every move.

'What are you doing, you little slag?' he hissed. 'What
do you think you're up to?'

I tried to get away from him but he dragged me back,
punching me in the stomach and kicking me in the shin.
He did that all the way home, punches and kicks, saying
the most awful, racist things to me, calling me someone
who loved mixed-race boys (I'm sure I don't have to say
the words, anyone reading this will know exactly what
those horrible phrases are), saying I was nothing more than
'meat' for black lads (but, again, using much worse names
for them), telling me I was a 'dirty n*gg*r shagger' for
what I was doing.

'Dad, I've done nothing wrong! Honest, I promise!' I
protested.

'You wouldn't know honesty if it punched you in the
face,' he sneered. 'Too busy shagging that type, aren't
you? Is that what you like? Is that what gets you going?'
With that, he whacked me across the side of the head and
I got a shattering pain in my ear. He kicked and punched
me all over and then, when we got home, he went into
my room and ripped up all my Elvis posters, smashed my
Elvis ornaments, knowing that was what would hurt me
more than what he did to my body. He burst my eardrum
that day and I was covered in bruises from top to bottom.

Looking back, I think he acted almost as if he was jealous, as if he genuinely thought we were a couple and I was cheating on him. He was my abuser but I think he believed he was protecting me from lads who would only want one thing from me, the one thing that he took all the time.

I'd never cry and I'd tell him that.

'You'll never see a tear from me, I'll never cry in front of you.'

'I'll break you,' he would say. 'I WILL break you.'

'You won't! You will never do that, you'll never see me cry over you and what you do to me,' I told him.

And I meant it – and I stuck to it. He had the power of raping me but he wouldn't have the power of seeing me upset.

The boy he'd caught me with – Mo – was just the friend of a friend and I'd honestly just cuddled him. I was terrified of the thought of any boy doing to me what my dad did, and desperate that they wouldn't find me attractive. Dad made sure that I knew everything that happened was my fault and I wanted to avoid that with any other boy or man for as long as I could.

'God, you're so beautiful!' he would tell me. 'Look at those long legs, look at that blonde hair! You're like an angel, you're gorgeous! I can't resist you – you know that, don't you? You know what you do to me?' Then he'd rape me.

I blamed myself for things I had no control over.

I wanted to be fat and ugly, but I know with hindsight that wouldn't have stopped him anyway, nothing would – I was completely trapped by my twisted father.

When the story of Josef Fritzl came out in later years, I felt a chill. That could have been me. If Keith Meadows could have locked me in a cellar for the rest of my life, he would have done so. If he'd killed me then, it would have been better. Everything he said, I had to do – the way I dressed, no make-up, I had to go everywhere with him – everything you could think of, there was no option. Mum never said a word. She never once said, *let her put a bit of lipstick on, let her come out with me for the day*. In all of those years, she was never a mother to me. She never once protected me, never loved me. It was as if she had resigned herself to everything – we were quite alike, I guess. We always did as we were told, but she rebelled through drink. About a year after he started abusing me, their fighting did calm down so maybe he left her alone, maybe she moved away from that side of their relationship now that I was fulfilling that role. It is beyond belief that she did that as a mother.

I used to start work at half past six in the morning, but one day I slept in.

'Why are you still in bed? You're a lazy bitch, aren't you? Always out shagging the boys, aren't you? That's why you can't get up on the morning,' Dad started yelling, banging around in my room. 'Get up now! Get to work!'

I got out of bed, dressed really quickly and put my overall on top of my clothes as he stood there. As soon as I was ready, he threw me on the bed, ripped my knickers off and lifted my legs up, spread them and raped me. I have always called that occasion rape, way before I was able to know that all of it was. It was violent and aggressive, and although everything else about the abuse was wrong, this time I really felt that he had done something way beyond his usual behaviour.

He put his hand in the pocket of his trousers and pulled out a pair of women's panties.

'Put these on,' he hissed.

I don't know whose they were as they weren't the sort that my mum usually wore, but lacy and fancy – and they were filthy. But I knew better than to challenge him, so meekly I put them on, sorted my clothes out and went to work, keeping them on until lunchtime in case he decided to check. They were absolutely disgusting, with the sort of stains on the crotch that come from sex, which makes me think that he must have been having sex with other women, still cheating on Mum. Also, it must have been premeditated: he had come into that room planning to rape me, to force me to wear those knickers or he wouldn't have had them in his pocket. This was all about anger.

By now, I was working mornings and nights for him as I'd left school at 16. I passed the rest of the time watching rubbish like *Sons and Daughters* on TV and cleaning the house. He'd come back every time he was on a break to check that I was there. I never escaped him. A lot was unsaid by then, but as a rule I would never have challenged him – I knew what he wanted and I knew what my life was, I knew what he expected and that there would be hell to pay if I did anything he didn't approve of. If I didn't stick by the unsaid rules, I was fully aware of what would happen.

Yet it was always at night. Daytime was for him saying things, telling me I was beautiful, promising we'd run away together. By the time we moved again to House Five, when I was 17, he was really laying it on thick about us running away together and getting married. I'd just brush it off – I didn't want to engage in his deluded fantasies but there was a part of me that thought, as I was getting older, would he actually do something about it? Would he force me to leave with him, to make a life with him? I could just be walking past him, going to my room, going to the bathroom and he'd whisper, 'One day we'll be together, you do know that? One day it'll just be us.'

He'd got a job working as a caretaker in a college which was why we moved again; this time he had a crew of men working under him and a gang of cleaners. A three-bedroom house came with the role and he went back into sharing a room with Mum – in single beds, which would mean she had no idea of him moving around in the middle of the night to come to me. I never thought that a new house would mean a new start, I just thought this was my life forever.

This was the house where the violence really ramped up. Headbutts were a way of life. If I said a single word he could take offence at, headbutt. Look at him the 'wrong' way, headbutt. Have an 'attitude', headbutt. He'd just walk off afterwards. It was a daily occurrence and he was always looking for a reason to hit someone. If Mum didn't do anything wrong, he'd find something I'd done – even though he'd made it up, or it was something tiny. With Mum, it was always about her drinking; for me, it could be anything, usually looking at him the wrong way.

By now, he was still raping me Monday, Wednesday, Friday and Sunday nights without fail. It was a routine, it was just what happened. I really had no hope of ever getting out of it. Someone else would have had to have seen what was going on as no one would believe me. And the one time someone did see, nothing happened.

It was Mum.

It was Mum who saw it was happening but she did nothing.

I was in my room in the new house and he was raping me – as usual. I think my mother must have got up to use the bathroom and I heard the door open once she was finished in there. I was over towards the wall and he was facing my back.

'I'm so sorry,' Dad muttered.

Was he talking to me? Why was he apologising to me? He'd never done that before. It took me a moment to realise there was someone else in the room with us – it was almost as if there was a time lapse in my brain before I processed what was going on and that my mother was standing there, watching her husband in bed with their daughter.

All she said as she witnessed him raping her child was, 'You've nothing to be sorry for, Keith, nothing whatsoever.' It was almost defiant towards me: there was blame in her voice, but it was directed at the wrong person.

She left the room, he got out of my bed and followed her. I waited for the shouting, I waited for them to fight – but there was nothing. It seemed as if they'd just gone back to bed and carried on as if it was all perfectly normal. How sick is that? Now I knew for sure that she was aware of what was going on, I knew my parents were colluding in my abuse. I'll never get over the fact that a mother can walk in on a father raping their daughter and do nothing. Even the fact that she said to him, 'You've nothing to be sorry for,' put all of the blame back on me. If it wasn't his fault, it was mine. Mum never walked in on us again. Well, why would she? She knew what she would see.

Now I was under no illusions. She wasn't coming to save me, she'd faced what was really going on and she'd chosen her side. And it wasn't the child who had been raped since she was a little girl, was it? I know that it will be hard for anyone who hasn't experienced abuse to read this and believe my story. It's beyond everything natural and right for a father to be doing those things to his child, but we still hold out hope for mothers, don't we? We believe that there is something in them that makes them look after their children, even protecting the ones not biologically linked to them, so when we come across a Rose West or a Lucy Letby or a Myra Hindley, it shocks us more – I think – than a man doing awful things. It's why a woman abusing kids or killing babies gets headlines in the way it does. It goes against nature. We hope that there's a goodness in women that will serve as an antidote to what so many men do and there is, there truly is in so many. But for some ... Well, they just don't seem to have that gene. My mother was one such woman – she was there for her man, even though he beat and degraded her, even though she knew he wasn't what he pretended to be – however, this was unforgivable.

Well, it certainly was for me. Now, I truly had no hope, nothing to hold on to. Dad wasn't going to change, and she wasn't going to stop him. I was completely and utterly alone.

Where Nightmares Begin

There are some things which take me back in an instant. I can remember the layout of my room so clearly; you'd walk in and there was a TV in the cabinet to the side, some drawers with a mirror on top at the side of that, and a boiler cupboard with the immersion heater in it, and my single bed. I got my first single in that house, 'Le Freak' by Chic, which Gram bought me. I was given a little record player in a case for Christmas and I spent so many hours in my room, dancing and singing, just trying to keep a different world alive. Those little things, the furniture, the few bits that were mine, were what I focused on when other things were going on with him.

When Dad was there, it was so very different and it tainted everything. He just did what he wanted to do and then left. But he still kept saying, 'We'll run away together, we'll get married.' It wasn't just when he was abusing me, I could be having a normal conversation with him during the day about what I'd did at school and he'd suddenly say, 'We'll get married soon, Mandy.' He was fixated on it, obsessed. As time went on, he was more confident, not just with talking about us running away together, but in trying to touch me. Mum was drunk most of the time and she'd spend the evenings ringing people up so that she could scream and shout at them.

'He's a bastard! I'm married to a bastard!' she'd yell dramatically, but it's odd, I do recall that she would also say, 'He's always hanging around young girls.' I sort of wondered if she was talking about me, but she never went into details. She'd seen him raping me, so maybe it was a reference to that, although it was hardly 'hanging around'. Maybe there were others; I'll never know.

But as time went on, even stranger things occurred. Mum wasn't the only one who was sectioned; it happened to Dad too. It seems so bizarre that not only was she subject to such an extreme thing, but he was as well. All I remember is some men coming for him in the middle of the night, I don't remember there being anything before that which suggested he was in a similar mental state to Mum or that something so drastic would happen. It's not as if being subjected to compulsory sectioning is a common thing – yet both of my parents went through it. The morning after it happened, Mum said that he had gone to a 'crazy hospital' and that was all that was mentioned until she took us all to the psychiatric unit to visit him later that day. It was all presented as something quite matter of fact: Dad had been taken away in the middle of the night, he'd been sectioned, and we'd be going to visit him somewhere as if it wasn't a big deal at all.

The place we went to was a locked ward and we had to wait for someone to let us in, but nothing else really registered with me. Dad was crying as he sat there in the day room, rocking back and forward, silently weeping. The rest of the people there were walking around in a daze, zombified, but Dad was in another world of his own – to me, it seemed as if he was play-acting, as if he was looking at the other people around him, taking bits from how they were behaving and putting them all together into his own version of what he should look like to other people. I was just relieved to have a week's respite from the abuse and couldn't really have cared less about what he was going through, whether it was real or made up.

When Dad was brought back by ambulance about a week later, Mum was standing at the door, swaying, while 'Welcome Home' by Peters and Lee played in the background. Still, nothing changed. It was to be a blip away from my 'normal'. He went straight back to abusing me the day after he got back. There were no tears from him then. It might sound harsh but I do think he was playing a game; he loved to be the centre of attention and maybe

Mum was getting too much of that attention and he didn't like it. I can't help but let my mind wander to something else as I write this – now that Mum had seen what he did, was there ever a part of him at that point that thought the game was up? If he pretended to be mad, would that help him if a report or allegation was ever made? He was such a conniving man that I wouldn't put it past him. His spell in a locked ward wasn't repeated – it was Mum who really struggled with poor mental health, not him. Her problems were much more obvious – phoning people, sending things in the post, being subjected to police visits, smashing glass – but she had no support for her condition as far as I could see and we were all just left to it in terms of social work involvement. I was certainly never aware of any visits checking up on us.

* * *

Everybody had to do as Dad said and life had to be just as he wanted it. He had to have the best clothes, a new Volvo parked outside (I think of them as 'nonce cars' now, I can't help it), particular meals at particular times. He had to have the best garden on the street, he always had to win at his bowling club, he just had to be top dog in everything.

My maternal grandad died when I was 16 and, for some reason, that made Dad say to me, 'I'll never touch you again, Mandy, not now your grandad's dead. I promise you that.' I wished on everything I had that it was true, but I didn't really believe him. That promise lasted a couple of days and I've no idea where it came from. Was it guilt that no one knew the true him? Or maybe a feeling that life's too short and you should try to be the best person you can be? Whatever brought it about, it passed as quickly as it came.

The abuse was repetitive, as if he had to go through a certain pattern each time to get what he wanted out of it. He never tried to make me say I was enjoying it, he just did it as if it was his right. For me, it wasn't just the horror of the abuse which I dreaded, it was the anticipation of it. My life became a sequence of the abuse happening and then just waiting for it to happen again. As soon as I realised it was his time for finishing work, my stomach would start to churn. If I had to go bowling with him, I would watch him to see if it was time to go home and for it to start. Even when we went to my paternal grandparents' caravan in Skegness, he raped me despite me being in a bunk bed with Fiona on top. That's how blatant he was. Mum was next door, my sister was above and he didn't care.

When I heard the door open, I knew it had to be him but could barely believe he would do it there. He pushed my nightie up, put himself into me, did what he needed to do and then left – he was shameless. The chances of getting caught didn't matter to him. Mum would be zonked out on medication and what would my sister do or say even if she did know what was going on?

He thought he was untouchable.

And, to me, it seemed that he was.

Four times a week, on his set nights, he would still come to my room. My nightmares would begin on those specific evenings, but they bled into every waking minute.

Dad was always laughing and joking, he didn't seem tortured – the opposite in fact, he acted as if he didn't have a care in the world. For the rest of that caravan holiday where he raped me in the bunk bed, I wore a long-sleeved jumper. No one said anything about me being covered up when I was on the beach, I was invisible to them. I was barely more than a child and worried that I was making myself too attractive; if I did that, then he'd do what he did. For decades I thought that, because no one ever said it wasn't my fault. I only had baths when he wasn't there – it made no difference. Mum questioned none of it.

She encouraged me to go with him. 'Oh God, I need a rest, Mandy! Go with your dad.' And did she know he was still abusing me? I always thought so – why would she think it was a one-off? Did she really convince herself that she'd happened to come into my room on the sole occasion he was raping me? That was some coincidence. As I've said before, I certainly always believed that while he was raping me, he was keeping away from her and that was something she wanted.

The rapes were still always at night-time. I just thought of it as him 'doing what he had to do' – that's how much

I minimised it and he normalised it. One summer evening, about 7 p.m., when I was 17, I was in my room listening to Elvis on the record player and singing along in my own little world, as usual. Dad stormed in.

'You're a lazy cow! Why can't you get up in the morning? Why do you lie in your pit until the last minute? It's disgusting, you're bone idle!'

Actually, the night before, I'd been allowed a friend to stay. I was given permission to be friends with Hazel as our mums knew each other, but he was never really happy about our friendship. One thing I remember is that Hazel was fantastic at cartwheels and he was always trying to get her to do them for him.

Any time she came, I'd say in advance, 'Don't do cartwheels if he asks you, Hazel, just don't.' I was so distrusting of him and was sure that he was getting some sort of sexual kick any time she did one. 'Oh, and I'll be wearing trousers, so you better too!' Again, it was my way of trying to keep other people safe – *don't draw attention to yourself, cover up, get past him as quickly as you can.*

'I've got to teach you a lesson,' he told me. 'Make sure you know that sort of behaviour is completely unacceptable. You're a lesbian, aren't you? Sleeping in the same bed as your friend last night. God knows what you were up to, but it wore you out, didn't it? Disgusting, lazy lesbian, that's what you are!' He was getting himself more and more worked up. 'You never listen, Mandy, you never listen.' With that, he threw me back onto the bed, ripped my knickers off, lifted my legs up, undid himself and raped me. 'Be up early in the morning,' he snapped as he left.

In my mind, that was 'proper rape'. It was incredibly rough and painful, and it was a different way of it happening, as well as it being light outside. But I still wouldn't tell anyone – I always thought I'd be taken away and the thought of that was worse than staying because it would be my fault. My sisters would go into care, my mother would kill herself, my dad would have his 'good name' taken, and it would all be because of me.

When I was about 17, and still cleaning the school where Dad was a caretaker, I was mopping up in the library one night. He came into the room and grabbed the mop from me.

'This is what I'm going to do,' he said, and started ramming the broom handle up inside me. I obviously had knickers on, but he just pushed those into me with the handle. He pushed with such violence, over and over again – and, on top of the pain, I was scared that time because someone could have walked in on us at any point. I don't know if he got any pleasure from it, but he just walked off when he'd had enough. When I was in the school, he would usually just touch me up whenever he wanted, even in front of other people, acting as if it was an accident and he'd bumped into me, but this was a step further than that.

I hated being anywhere near him, I felt physically sick

and kept as far away as possible but he created situations where we had to be together, whether it was overtime or something else. He never raped me in the school, but he got damned near to it. He worked in a few schools and one of them had a swimming pool. I remember one day Dad took all three of us girls there and while the others splashed about, he told me he'd teach me to swim.

'Just lie there and float,' he said. His hands were under me, holding me by my boobs and my moo with my sisters right there beside me. He was gliding me through the water with his hands over my private parts, pressing his fingers in. Then, as always, he just decided that it was over and stopped. I still can't swim. It's interesting that he never went under my clothes in public places like that as it showed he did have boundaries, he did know what he was doing, otherwise he'd have just been abusing me in the street, wouldn't he?

He used to bring other caretakers to the house for get-togethers and I would think, *dear God, he's going to make me do things with them*. It never happened but it was a feeling I had, not just from the pornography he had shown me with orgies in the films, but just the sense that he could do anything he wanted at any time. He knew I was petrified of him and he played on it.

One night, he pulled his coat on and said, 'Right, Mandy, let's go to the pub.'

'I don't want to, I'm happy here,' I told him.

'Tough! Your mum's at the caravan, so let's go out for a drink.'

I had to do as I was told so I got my jacket and went in the car with him. In the first one, everyone knew him – as usual.

'Oh, who have you got here then, Keith? This your eldest?' They all knew who I was but it was that sort of meaningless chat you get in such places.

'You'll have to keep an eye on her!'

'Get your hand in your pocket then, Keith – buy her a drink!'

We stayed there for a couple of drinks then moved on to another one, where he kept trying to get me to drink more and more. I drank as little as I could and we soon moved on to another pub, where there was a sort of disco on.

'Cuddle up to me,' he demanded in the next place.

'No, I'm not doing that!'

'Hold my hand then.'

'No, I'm not doing that either.' He sighed in frustration, scanning the room as if he was thinking about what to do next. 'Dance with him,' Dad said to me, quietly, nodding towards a man in the corner.

'What? That old man?' He was probably about 40 but that was ancient to me.

'Do it – dance with him.'

Again, I had to do it, and there was nothing weird about

the bloke, he just had a little cheery dance with me, there wasn't any touching, but as soon as we got home, Dad changed after not saying a word in the car.

'You slag! You absolute slag! I bet you're going to sneak away and meet him, aren't you? You're going to have sex with him, aren't you?'

'Of course not – why would I do that?'

'I know what you are, I know!'

I went upstairs to get away from him but as soon as I got in my bedroom, he was behind me, pushing me down on the bed. He pulled my jeans and knickers off, all the while telling me I was a slag. He seemed driven that night and it was much more forceful. He'd created the situation, blamed me when it happened, then obviously became aroused by it.

'You're stupid, Mandy, so stupid! This is why I have to do this – you know that, don't you? You never learn and I'm the only one who can teach you.'

I'd only done as I was told – as usual – but I could never do right, which was weird given that he was still constantly talking about us running away together. The pub night must have been part of that boyfriend and girlfriend fantasy. Mum was out of town and even though most people knew Dad, there might be a few strangers in the bars who would think we were a couple.

I worked in a chip shop round about that age as well as cleaning, which gave me a bit of an excuse for going

out and escaping him. Mum got me the job after seeing
an advert in their window and when I started, Dad could
pop in whenever he wanted to check that I was working
there. Gloria, who owned the shop, also asked me if I could
help out by cleaning her house. That was a great excuse
for me because if Dad ever looked in the window and
didn't spot me there, I would get dog's abuse when I went
home but now I could say he just didn't see me because
I was cleaning.

I had a little Post Office account, which became my
secret running away fund, and all the money from my job
went in there but I had no plans to escape, it was just a
vague notion that I hoped would happen one day – I still
wanted someone to save me. When I was 19, I had a secret
boyfriend – not for long though, the only thing that was
ever secret to the world was what Dad did to me. The only
place I was allowed to go was to a friend's house, even at
that age, and only on rare occasions with the instruction
that I had to be back within the hour. That was where
I first met Dan. I was also allowed to go to the shop for
sweets or chocolate; it was there and at a park where I used
to meet him. He worked at a garage and I'd call his work
and tell him what time I'd be there, arranging our time
together like a secret mission.

Dad had lost his job and so we'd moved by this time.
We were now living in a maisonette that was higher up
than the ground that the park was on and Dad used to

look out onto the park a lot. I can only assume that's what he was doing one day when he saw me and Dan. I knew nothing about it at first, we said goodbye and I went home, walking straight in and sitting down.

'Where have you been?'

'Nowhere.'

'That's a lie.'

'I was at the shop.'

'That's a lie too.'

'Don't lie to your father,' Mum chipped in.

'I saw you, I was watching you – you were with a boy.' He came over to the sofa and started screaming in my face. 'You're nothing but a slag, aren't you? Going out with the likes of him, going out with P*kis – you'll get a name for yourself, but you don't care, do you? Slag, slag, slag!'

I got up to get away from him and he grabbed me. There were concrete steps with metal strips on them outside our door and as I went out of the door, he pushed me and I fell. He got hold of my legs and dragged me all the way down the steps as I screamed, 'I'm bleeding, Dad, you've hit my head! I'm bleeding, I'm really hurt!'

'Shut up, slag, there's nothing wrong with you!' he snapped.

I had a massive gash on my head and Mum, who was watching behind him, finally interrupted and said, meekly, 'She'll maybe need to go to hospital with that, Keith.'

'No! She's not going anywhere near hospital, she's fine.'

He did let me go then and I ran back inside, into the bathroom, where I washed the blood off and pressed a towel to the side of my head – where I can still see the scar even now. I knew that there was no point in asking if I could go to hospital, it would never have been allowed as someone might have asked questions. This was something visible, something outsiders might look at and dig a little deeper, and I'd pay the price for even suggesting that I seek help. I tried to push the sides of the gash together with the towel and just hoped it would heal enough by itself for me to just get on with things as usual.

When Dad felt that his perverted relationship with me was being challenged, his violence seemed to know no bounds, but I was getting older and needed some freedom even if home remained the hell it always was.

Dan was actually the first boy I had sex with and to me, in my head, it was the first time I'd actually had sex with anyone – I didn't think of what Dad did to me as the same thing at all. That was disgusting, that was wrong. However, he'd ruined me so much that I couldn't enjoy it with Dan. I used to just do it because he wanted to, which wasn't much of a difference really, was it? I'd just lie there, no enjoyment, and it didn't feel any different apart from him kissing me. It was an exchange – if he liked me, I would do the things I didn't want to do. As with Dad, I just took myself out of it. My mind went somewhere else as I allowed a man to use my body in whatever way he chose. From the first time we did 'that' to the last, I never engaged; I never even tried to be in the moment, I just went along with it. Was it rape too? No, I wouldn't say so, because I could have left – I could have stopped it, I think – but there certainly wasn't any pleasure in it, there was nothing for me, I was something to be used. The movements were the same, the pressure of Dan's body on mine was the same, the only difference was that he kissed me – which I didn't particularly like anyway as it was just the start of him trying to do what he wanted.

I kept seeing Dan for a week or two even after Dad dragged me down the steps. As long as he didn't see me with a boy, he would leave me alone; but if he did, the red mist would descend and I would be battered senseless. It wasn't worth it, it wasn't worth trying to meet a lad and have a normal relationship, especially given that I was going through the motions anyway. I couldn't see anything changing – unless Dad killed me.

7

Ben

I never planned to tell. I'd never thought I would be brave enough because, even at the age of 19, I thought it would all come back on me. I'd be blamed, I'd be the one who was shunned.

There was a girl I knew from school who was fostered out to her auntie, a girl called Debbie. Her auntie – a lovely woman called Rose – always made me welcome and we kept up our friendship even though I'd left school a few years ago. I'd just hang around Rose's house, chatting to both her and Debbie, feeling comfortable and safe. Dad wasn't bothered about me being there – I guess it didn't seem threatening to him as there were no boys around and that was what bothered him more than anything. I did, however, always have to be back early evening. I wasn't allowed to stay over.

I think I must have just been feeling that there was such a different atmosphere in Rose's house and that I could be open with Debbie because, out of nowhere, it came out.

'Debbie – my dad does things to me,' I said.

'What?' she barely bothered to drag her eyes from the TV. 'What do you mean he does "things" to you?'

'Just that – he does things to me.'

'He beats you up, doesn't he? I've seen bruises on you for years.'

'Yeah … but that's not what I meant. I meant that, well, he touches me.'

She was paying attention now. 'Where? Where does he touch you?'

'Everywhere. All over my body, my moo, everywhere.'

'Christ, Mandy! That's hideous! What if he went further?'

Now that I had started, I had to admit it: 'He does go further. Debbie, he does everything.'

'Everything?'

'Yeah – he makes me have sex with him.'

Everything went silent, then she shouted, 'Auntie Rose! Auntie Rose!' Rose came flying through from the other room, probably thinking there had been an accident and asked what was going on.

'Can I tell her?' Debbie asked. I shrugged. It was out now. 'You know Mandy's dad?' she asked her auntie.

'Of course I do. What's he done?' she said, narrowing her eyes.

Debbie glanced over at me. 'Oh God, Auntie Rose – he's been interfering with Mandy. He's been touching her. He's been making her have sex with him.'

It felt weird hearing those words coming from someone else's mouth and knowing they were about me. I'd kept quiet for eight years, and yet now I was sitting in a cosy front room with one of my few friends while she told her auntie my deepest, darkest secret. Rose was quiet, very quiet, and I started to feel worried that she'd tell us to stop mucking about. Instead, she came over, took my hand and said, 'You're staying here tonight, Mandy love.'

Rose contacted Social Services, who agreed that I should stay there overnight and that they would get the police involved. I knew that everything had been set in motion and that I'd done the very thing I'd been warned against for years, but Rose's support meant the world to me. When Dad realised that it was late and I didn't seem to be coming back, he turned up at her door.

Banging on it, he roared, 'Mandy! Get out here now and get home! I won't tell you twice.'

Rose shouted in reply, 'Piss off, you disgusting man because I'll fucking kill you if you don't! She's not coming back, she's not coming back after all you've done to her.'

Those words must have been enough for him to realise the can of worms had been opened because, surprisingly, he did leave and I did stay with Rose and Debbie that night. I couldn't sleep, not just with all the questions Debbie was throwing at me, but because I wondered whether I had finally done it. Would the police believe me? Would I be put somewhere safe now that I was 19? Surely I was too old to go into something like foster care? I allowed myself a little fantasy that I would be given a flat where I could live in peace, forging a life for myself, getting a job that had nothing to do with my father, maybe even being happy.

In the morning, I did all the normal things like getting dressed and eating the toast Rose had made for me, but I was waiting for that knock on the door, which finally came. A social worker took me to the police station without asking many questions, just having a general chat, but as soon as I got to the station, I knew that my little fantasy was never going to come true.

The officer who came to the desk looked at me in barely disguised disgust.

'Meadows?' he said to the social worker. 'Meadows, you say?' She nodded and I thought, *you know my dad, don't you? You know him from the Specials.* 'We'll deal with it now,' he told her. The social worker smiled at me as she left but I wasn't taken in for an interview, the officer just came out from behind the desk and said, 'Let's get you home.'

I don't know how he knew where she lived but he and a colleague took me to Gram's house. In the kitchen, they told her everything, while I listened from the living room, hearing snatches of their conversation.

Lot of nonsense.

She's obviously got it in for her dad.

No, it'll all work out but you need to have a word with her.

Just as they left, Fiona appeared at the door, wet through from the rain – she came in and said, 'Dad's been arrested for something! You'll have to come, Gram – Mum needs you.'

'Mandy!' shouted Gram and I walked through to the kitchen. 'Listen to me. I don't know what you think you're doing, but if this goes any further, your mum will never be able to cope. Please tell them you were lying, Mandy, please tell them it was all a lie. Please tell them it's not true. It'll ruin everything.'

Even you, Gram? I thought. *Even you?*

Phone calls were made and one of my posh aunties, a Jehovah's Witness who didn't have much to do with us, turned up. No one said anything else – I was just taken in her car, back to the police station.

I knew what I had to do.

'I lied about it all,' I said. 'I was pissed off with everyone so I made it up.'

They put me in a cell and I had to wait for a sergeant to be free. When he came, I was taken into an interview room and he said, 'Mandy Meadows, I'm cautioning you for wasting police time. You'll have your photos and fingerprints taken and they will remain on record.'

That's exactly what happened. They treated me like a criminal and didn't ask a single question. I was terrified that I had a police record now – I still am after all these years.

My posh auntie drove me back to Gram and I said, 'I've done it. I've told them it was a lie so everything can just go back to how it was.'

'Even if it did happen, Mandy, let's just forget about it,' she told me, looking pissed off rather than actually concerned that her granddaughter had said her own father was abusing her. I think that hurt more than almost anything. This was the woman who had been my guiding light for me, she had loved me in her own way and she had looked out for me over the years with a devotion no one else had ever come close to, and now she was dismissing one of the biggest things someone can ever disclose. *Let's just forget about it*. I wanted to scream, 'Yes, you do that! But me? No, I don't think I'll be forgetting about it. I don't think I'll be forgetting about it for the rest of my life, Gram.' Of course, I said nothing as another shard of betrayal entered my heart.

When I went home, my parents were both furious – Dad wouldn't even speak to me. Mum was ranting and raving, still pretending it wasn't the truth even though she had seen it with her own eyes years earlier. She went off to get pissed and Dad sidled over to me as soon as she was out the door.

'I told you this is what would happen, didn't I? I told you. Who's going to believe you? No one. No one at all.'

He was more confident than ever after that and the social workers didn't follow up on anything, they just all accepted I'd lied.

* * *

Nothing really happened for the next year or so – the rapes, the abuse stayed the same – but then there was a change. I met a lad called Billy who lived in a bedsit above a shop, which was an absolute shithole. I think that was just his place for seeing girls as I later found out he was married. Billy was about five years older than me and it felt just the way it had with my last boyfriend. I was only having sex because he wanted to, there was no pleasure in it for me but I should have been paying more attention, I should have been thinking about things more.

I had a cold and was on antibiotics, which I know now makes the Pill less effective. My period stopped and I just knew. I was only 20 years old and facing up to the most horrific thing imaginable – all I could hold on to was the hope it was Billy's baby.

Despite everything, Mum was the first person I turned to.

'How can you be pregnant, you stupid cow?' she sneered. 'You haven't even got a boyfriend.'

'It was somebody I met one day.'

'Where? You don't go anywhere.'

I didn't say that I wasn't *allowed* to go anywhere. 'At a friend's house.'

'A "friend"? Who would be friends with you?'

I shrugged, the insults raining off my back as usual.

'And he's made you pregnant?'

'I think so,' I confirmed.

Sighing, Mum said, 'Right, we better do a pregnancy test then.' She went into the bathroom and came back with one of her empty tablet bottles. Handing the brown screw-top container to me, she sighed again. 'Piss into this and we'll take it to the chemist.'

I did as I was told and she went into town with it on her own.

A couple of hours later, she came back a changed woman. When I saw the smile on her face, I honestly thought it must have been because she was relieved that it was negative. Instead, she grabbed me by the arms and squealed, 'Ooh, I'm going to be a grandma!'

This woman had already seen me being raped by my father – her husband – but she seemed to have managed to put that out of her mind. To be honest, I was the same because I never thought that your dad could get you pregnant, it seemed a ludicrous idea so it must be Billy's. I'd been so secluded. I was naïve and quiet, I truly thought it would be impossible for a young girl to have a baby with her own father.

Mum was on the ceiling with excitement, hugging me

and jumping around. When Dad came in, she couldn't wait to tell him.

'Guess what, Keith? Go on, guess!'

'No. If you've got something to say, then say it.'

'We're going to be grandparents!' she said in a stupid singsong voice. 'Can you imagine? Mandy's having a baby!'

Looking at me, all he said was, 'Oh. Is she?'

He must have known, how could he not?

Mum was all over me – she would sit beside me, she wanted to go everywhere with me to buy baby clothes and things like that. She told me about her labour and terrified me by saying I'd need an enema! She was what a mother should be for the first time in my life.

It made no difference to Dad's behaviour though; he kept raping me. Every Monday. Every Wednesday. Every Friday. Every Sunday. He was like clockwork. I'd missed two periods so wasn't that far on but Mum got me registered for maternity care at Halifax General as soon as the GP confirmed my pregnancy. I don't think there was a single emotion I didn't feel. Terrified that I was pregnant at all. Ashamed that it might be my father's. Horrified at what people would think. Frightened that an innocent baby was being brought into the hell that was our home. Panicked that I would have to give birth at all. And underneath it all I was pregnant to my paedophile father; what would he do to a baby that we had made together through his disgusting perversions?

As soon as Mum found out I was pregnant, she told Gram. She practically flew into the house on a cloud of happiness after that conversation.

'I've told your gram you're pregnant and she's disgusted! She can't believe you've done this, Mandy – she can't believe that you'd bring a child into this world and it will be having just the same life as she did, born illegitimate, born a bastard! She doesn't want anything to do with you. Don't go near her, she won't speak to you.' It was like a dagger to my heart. I was speechless but I took her at her word and kept away.

It was such an odd, tight relationship with my mum from the start of that pregnancy. She was the excited granny-to-be and I was the daughter she'd always wanted. Although she was happy to call me names when she was reporting from other people, like Gram, she was nicer to me than she'd ever been before. It's hard to understand as she must have known the baby was Dad's – she'd come in on us in that room and I always suspected she colluded. I admit, even though it was twisted, I loved the way that relationship was with her in those days; she only ever drank once that I can remember in the whole pregnancy. I was just so desperate for love that I didn't care where it came from – I had a real mum for the first time in my life. Dad abused me throughout though, nothing changed there, although he had stopped showing me the pornographic and bestiality videos by then, more because the video shop had closed than anything else, I think.

My body had never been my own and now there was something growing in me that was completely outlandish – I felt fat, bloated, it was all so strange. It looked like an alien moving in me and I was freaked out, but I wouldn't say I had any connection to my unborn child. Mum loved it all, the whole pregnancy made her happy and animated in a way I'd never seen before. I was so tiny that you could see all the baby's features when it moved and she'd point out the feet, the hands and things like that, touching me, making a connection that had never existed between us at any other point.

I convinced myself that the chances of the baby being Billy's were 50/50. I also thought that a father couldn't get his daughter pregnant. I'd never heard of anything like that until one day, I saw a story in a magazine. Mum had some magazines lying around and one of the front pages screamed, *PERVERT! MY DAD MADE ME PREGNANT!* I was horrified to see that this could happen. I left it lying around for Dad to see.

'Is this for me?' he asked later that day, waving the magazine in my face.

'Yeah, it is,' I muttered.

'Well, I'm not a pervert. I love you. I'm not a paedophile, am I?'

With that, he walked away and threw the magazine in the bin. Just seeing that story was a bit of reality for me. It could happen, I just prayed it wasn't going to happen to me.

I went into premature labour when I was five months pregnant and had to undergo a lot of blood tests. When Dad knew about that, he kicked off.

'They're going to find out,' he said. 'They're going to find out this baby's mine. What'll happen then?' he asked, as if I had the answers to everything. 'What am I going to do? You know you'll get taken away, don't you, Mandy? You know the baby will get taken away? And, oh God, I'll go to prison – how will your mother cope? This is the end, this is the end!'

I completely ignored him. I'd never seen him panic like that but I'd be damned if I was going to offer any comfort. Anyway, I was still holding on to the hope that Billy was the father. I had told him, but he wasn't interested.

'I think I'm pregnant,' I finally admitted one day.

'You can't be, you just can't be.'

'Well, I am. We haven't been using anything, so it was always something that could happen.'

'I don't need this, Mandy – we're done.'

And that was that.

* * *

Mum and I were in a café one day and she was sitting nearest to the window.

'Look,' I said, 'that's the lad who's the dad. That's Billy.'

She knocked loudly on the window and shouted, 'WE WANT SOME MONEY FOR THE BABY!' He ignored her and carried on walking. Mum didn't say anything about him being black, she just shouted that I needed money from him and that was that. Even though they were racist, bizarrely they weren't as bad with black people; they saved their hatred for other groups. I suppose on seeing Billy, she would have thought the baby would be mixed-race, but she never once referred to it. I certainly didn't have anything to do with him once I was pregnant, but I did hold on to the hope that the baby would be his rather than Dad's and I knew I would of course be able to tell from the colour as soon as the baby was born.

I felt nothing about the baby when I was pregnant but told myself it was because I was so busy being sick for the whole nine months, morning, noon and night. Mum was beside me all the time – the best mother ever. We'd walk arm in arm through town, she'd treat me to little things; it was the relationship I'd always hoped for and I'd only got it through my own father making me pregnant.

I had another scare at six months when we were at the caravan in Skegness. It was during the night and I got this overwhelming urge to go to the loo. When I got there, I could feel myself wanting to push.

'Mum!' I shouted. There wasn't much room in the caravan so she was there instantly. 'I want to push, I really want to push!'

'Well, you can't! Hold on, Mandy, your dad needs to get you to hospital.'

It was just a little village place and they blue-lighted me to a major hospital. I was in there for a day for monitoring before it settled down a bit and then I went home. I wasn't given any special treatment and I kept on with my cleaning jobs until I was seven months, then my high blood pressure got worse and I developed pre-eclampsia, a dangerous condition that causes high blood pressure, which meant I had to stop as my feet were so swollen. I also had protein in my urine and I could have been in a really bad way at any point, so they had to be ready to deliver. Dad went with me to every antenatal appointment, sitting at the side of me, watching to see what was going on.

'I'll always be by your side, Mandy,' he would whisper. 'And this baby – well, this baby will call me Daddy.'

He still raped me after that but I never said a word – why would I? I'd tried before and look how that had turned out.

By then I was getting monitored for pre-eclampsia every week and they decided to induce me a couple of weeks early. I was put on a drip but nothing happened for ages. Dad had been with me to every appointment and he was there for the induction too, sitting next to me on the uncomfortable chair next to what seems to be every bed in hospital wards – waiting for the birth of his child.

They decided to break my waters and he found that hilarious. 'It's like a swimming pool in here, Mandy!' he laughed and all the midwives joined in.

What a great guy he was.

I stared at the clock, watching the hands move, terrified about what was coming. They gave me a cervical sweep and I was in labour pretty quickly after that. I was only in actual labour for an hour or so, with my baby coming out at a minute past midnight ...

On my 21st birthday.

A boy called Ben.

A completely, unmistakably little white boy.

Dear Mandy

I know you thought you'd never get out – and writing this, why would you entertain even the slightest hope? You're a prisoner, you're being held against your will and you're now the mother of your own father's child. I've wanted to reach out to you at so many points of this story but I remember the darkness of this moment as you looked at Ben, as you looked at his skin and *knew*.

There wasn't a hint of doubt really, was there? And I think at that point, you truly believed your life would be as nothing but a baby mill for Keith Meadows. He had the son he always wanted and he couldn't have been happier. Why would he stop now? He'd got away with it, he'd even been caught by his own wife, so why not go on? Have more babies, keep telling you that you'd run away together, make plans for this to be your destiny.

I also remember the numbness which came from having no emotional response to the tiny baby who had just come from your shattered body. No joy, no elation, no rush of motherly obsession – but I also know that there was an immediate need to protect that little boy from his father. And what is that but maternal love? What is that but a basic, primitive knowing that there are monsters out there and sometimes it is only us broken women who can fight them?

A child born from rape is still a child. They are innocent, they are pure and you knew that all along, you knew it from the moment Ben was born. However, I know you'll be hard on yourself, I know you'll question whether you should even be called a mother, but motherhood comes in many forms. It doesn't always fit in with fairy-tale images, it can be heavy and splintered, heart-breaking and thankless, but it can grow and your love for this scrap of a boy will do that, and in that love, you'll find what it takes to get out.

8

This is Your Life Now

There was no doubt in my mind that the baby wasn't Billy's. This child was clearly completely white, which meant that there was only one other option: my father had just watched his own child being born to his daughter.

'Pass him to Grandad!' said the midwife as she prepared to stitch me up. 'Oh look! Look how proud he is!'

And he was – he was deliriously happy.

Get off my baby, I thought. *Get your hands off him, he's mine.* But what could I do? I knew immediately I would never have a bond with this baby because it was his. I felt nothing for him, I felt my baby was soiled.

'Oh look, son!' Dad said. 'You're in the world now, son!'

Son. He was calling him 'son'.

'He's called Ben,' I snapped.

'That sounds like a dog – name him something better than that.'

'No, his name is Ben. Call him that.' I just wanted the 'son' nonsense to stop.

I didn't breastfeed; I didn't really want any contact with the baby. He was with me in a side ward for about four days until he got really bad jaundice and it was discovered he had a heart murmur. He didn't want his feeds and was just incredibly sleepy, such a floppy baby. Ben was put under a light in Special Care and I was told that he would need a blood transfusion if the jaundice didn't get better. Dad was there whenever he could be – he was affectionate and caring, and he was still calling him 'son'. He basically took over, asking the doctors all the questions, and again looked as if he was a fantastic person, watching out for his feckless daughter and her baby.

We eventually got home once Ben was a bit better, round about when he was two weeks old, but he was constantly poorly. He had chest infections all the time and I was never away from the GP. I kept Ben in my bedroom with me but it didn't stop Dad. He was back at me, raping me, within a fortnight. It sounds crazy, but I was expecting it. Even though I'd just given birth and was still sore, I knew he'd soon come to my room and abuse me. I didn't think he would ever stop actually, I was under no illusions – if I was living there, he'd do it. I was in agony from the stitches, but he didn't care. I bled horrifically the first time he raped me after Ben, but he dismissed it.

'You'll be fine, stop moaning – women know how to deal with these things,' he told me as he left my room.

Still, there was never a tear from me. I might be bruised, I might be in agony and bleeding, but he wouldn't get a single tear from me, he wouldn't get that satisfaction.

In the morning, I had to tell Mum I was bleeding.

'Why? What have you been doing?'

'Nothing! I'm only ever with the baby, I don't do anything,' I protested.

'Oh God, you'll be fine – sit on that rubber ring they gave you and get on with things, stop moaning,' she told me.

So, I did; I got on with it as I always did. When I went back to get the stitches out, I just hoped someone would notice they had been burst but no one said anything. I was a fool to think anyone would ever notice anything, ever.

By December, I felt I was more at the GP and hospital than away from them. I felt sorry for Ben as I was spending more time with him by myself but it wasn't the sort of maternal bond it should be; it was as if I was holding someone else's child. I wanted him to get better because who wouldn't want that for any baby? However, I didn't want it because I adored him and my world turned around him. He was just a sick child and no one wants that. Of course I feel hugely guilty about that now, and I think I always will, but I have to be truthful here and I hope that a lot of other women who have children conceived from rape will feel grateful that someone can voice these thoughts – he was a baby who needed so much but I could only focus on the practical stuff as there simply wasn't any emotional connection there at that point.

Any time he was in hospital, I felt safe. I could stay with him – in fact, if I could have stayed there forever, I would have done so. The medical visits were non-stop and after one emergency appointment at the GP when he was three months old and his lips were purple, I was told that Ben was in heart failure and that he had to get treatment immediately. He was transferred to a heart hospital in Leeds and I was told he had a hole in his heart.

'It closes in some babies fairly quickly,' the doctor said, 'but, sadly, that hasn't happened with Ben. We would usually do a procedure where we put a balloon into his heart to see if we can close the hole but we think it will be best in this case to just monitor him and see what happens.'

I just had to hope that they were making the right decision and that in choosing to monitor Ben rather than do an operation, he wouldn't get any worse. But as time went on, the floppiness wasn't getting any better, Ben clearly wasn't thriving. Dad was in pieces and when he had to leave us both in Leeds that first night, he was horrified to be told he wouldn't be able to stay as men weren't allowed to sleep over in those days. I was given a little room in accommodation that had been for nurses years ago but I was shocked the next day when Fiona turned up.

'What are you doing here?' I asked.

'I'm not really sure,' my sister admitted. 'Dad told me that I had to come.'

'Why?'

She shrugged in a non-committal way but I knew what he was doing – he was scared that I might have some freedom, he must have genuinely thought that I would be off having a good time while my baby was being kept in hospital. He needed to keep me on a leash even then.

Mum had taken over from the moment I had Ben. One morning I slept in and when I woke up, he was gone. She'd taken him out of the cot and left for a walk. When she came back, she snapped, 'You can't look after this baby, Mandy. You're useless! This is your life now, you're a mother – but you're shit at it!'

That's all I heard: *Useless. Rubbish. Crap.*

Even when we knew there was something wrong with Ben, my parents both mollycoddled him constantly. I guess that it's natural, most people would do that with a baby who was facing problems, but they had no interest in trying to find out what would help Ben. They just wrapped him in cotton wool and wouldn't even do the stretching exercises that he needed to do from the moment he was born in the hope that his muscles could be built up and he'd be less floppy. It was as if they wanted him to be totally dependent on them whereas I always felt that, given the chance, I would crack on with everything that was advised and hopefully give Ben some chance. They wouldn't even do the normal things that you do with babies, like giving them tummy time to encourage them to roll over or make their necks stronger. I put him in a bouncy chair one day and Mum came hurtling through from the kitchen.

'What are you doing? His legs can't take that! Get him out right now!' she said, lifting him.

'He'll be fine – his legs don't need to do anything in it, he's supported.'

'He is not! You can't put a baby like Ben in something like that. You've got no idea, Mandy, no idea at all.'

'He's different,' they always insisted. 'You can't do anything, so we'll take him.'

I don't doubt for a minute that they loved him, but I think they also enjoyed the opportunity to stick the knife in me.

Whenever I went to the baby clinic on a Friday, I could see that the other little ones born at the same time were making so much progress, but Ben was stuck. He was still in and out of hospital all the time too. Mum hated that I was recognised as Ben's mum there and that I was treated as a mother, not as a stupid little girl. She was always furious when I stayed over at the hospital and the next time it was an option when he was about six or seven months, she dictated to me, 'I'm the one who's staying with Ben tonight, I'm more of a mother to him than you are.'

'Don't be stupid, Mum,' I told her. 'You dose yourself up on sleeping pills every night. You'd be in no condition to look after Ben if he needed anything.'

'You can shut up and piss off!' she snapped. 'I've told you, I'm staying.'

No doubt the medical staff thought she was being a fantastic granny, helping out her exhausted single mum daughter, but their delusions must have been shattered when she fell asleep with Ben in her arms, dopey on Valium, and dropped him on the floor. The nurses took him off her and she went mad; the only thing they could do was kick her out. She wangled her way back in for the next meeting with the consultant but was never allowed to stay over again. Ben was about eight months at this point and the staff had managed to set up another appointment, this time with a paediatrician.

'We're going to have to do some tests,' the new doctor told me. 'We think Ben might have Down's syndrome.'

Their suspicions had been raised because of the thickness of the skin on the back of his neck, but the results all came back negative – he was just born that way.

'He'll be a late developer,' I was informed. 'He might not walk until he's two or three, who knows?'

But I didn't believe them. I think deep down I knew he was my father's child, but I tried to deny it and said to myself that these things just didn't happen. I still thought, surely there was no way a man could make his own daughter pregnant? Maybe Billy just had a skin colour that wasn't too strong, maybe my genes had beaten his. I held on to every shred of hope there was.

Dad was still calling him 'son', but in a way that he could get away with. It's hard to explain, I guess, but if he said, 'There you go, son, there's a good lad,' I knew he was actually referring to him as his own flesh and blood, whereas other people would no doubt just think he was using the word as a version of 'good lad' or something like that.

I felt as if I was going to scream every time I heard him say it and one day I finally exploded: 'Can you stop doing that?' I shouted. 'Just stop it, stop saying that he's your son!'

'Why?'

'I just don't like it.'

'Well, he'll be talking soon and he'll call me Daddy then so why can't I call him "son"?'

My blood ran cold.

'He will not, he will NOT call you Daddy!'

But he just smirked at me. 'He will, Mandy. That's what he'll say. He'll always call me Daddy.'

It had been such a big thing for me to defy my father, to actually say no and stand up to him, but it seemed every time he spoke to Ben after that, he'd say something like, 'Here's your daddy,' or 'Come to Daddy, Ben'. It sounds heartless but I'm glad that Ben never ended up speaking for years as it would have killed me to hear him say those words. I'm sure anyone else would have just thought it was part of good old Keith Meadows being a great guy. His slag of a daughter had a kid to someone she wasn't even with and there he was supporting them both *and* acting like a real dad to the poor child. Any time I asked him to stop referring to himself that way, he just laughed.

'He'll call me Daddy because anything else will confuse him. You girls call me that and I don't want him to feel left out – why wouldn't he call me Daddy?' he asked me, staring in defiance, knowing full well what he was really saying.

I'd gone back to work for Dad quite quickly after having Ben and that meant that he was back to having access to me there as well. Mum would go to the static caravan for the 'season' and she had a job working in one of the arcades; I took Ben there too, where I had a part-time job at the chip shop. Being with her was always awful, but at least I escaped from Dad for two months. That was until Ben got really severe gastroenteritis and the local GPs told me to take him back home to his usual doctors.

I did go home and Ben got better – well, as better as he could – and life went back to 'normal'. One day I was in town with Ben, having a coffee with my sister, Fiona, when she pointed out a lad that she knew: 'That's Pete,' she told me as he walked towards us.

'Hiya, Talk-a-lot,' he said to her. 'Feeling chatty today?'

It turned out that was what he always called her as she was such a little mouse who never really said anything to lads.

'Who's this, then?' he asked, nodding towards me. 'Your mum?'

'Cheeky!' she finally spoke. 'It's my sister, Mandy.'

And that was it. That was the change in my life. This lad Pete was wearing an Everton scarf and sweatbands on his wrists for some reason. He got a cup of tea and sat down beside us.

'Got any matches?' he asked.

'No.'

'Got a lighter?'

'No.'

It was riveting stuff but at least I was brave enough to talk to him! He chatted to Fiona about someone they knew – although she didn't say much – and when he left, I just thought, *he's nice.*

'How do you know him?' I asked Fiona.

'He's sometimes at my mate's house when I go,' she told me.

'Oh, is he? Maybe I'll come with you one day.'

I liked him straight away, this funny little dark-haired bloke with dark skin and something about him. I can't say he was my sort as I'd never had a sort before – I wasn't allowed. I found myself thinking about him a lot, it was the fact that he'd made me laugh quite a bit just in the 10 minutes or so we'd been together in the café. I needed that in my life, but I should have known nothing would be easy.

Pete was about five years older than me but he seemed really worldly because he was confident, and that was something I couldn't imagine being.

'Do you fancy him?' Fiona asked me later.

'Well ... he's all right, isn't he?'

'But, Mandy – he's ... he's Asian!' she exclaimed.

'What difference does that make?'

'It's not right.'

'What are you talking about? You're the one with a problem if that's what you think. He's a nice lad, funny. Yeah, I like him.'

I started going to Fiona's friend's house and that was allowed because I was with her, I wasn't on my own. Everyone would just be sitting round, it wasn't exciting. Fiona's mate had a kid, who I played with, and Pete messed about with her partner, who had a motorbike.

'You don't say much, do you?' he'd tease. 'I think I'll start calling you Talk-a-lot's Mum.'

One day he asked me to go for a walk with him and he said, 'I think I like you – do you want to see me again?'

Inside my heart was racing, but I just casually replied, 'Yeah, OK.'

When I went back to Fiona, I warned her to cover for me if anyone noticed I'd been away for a bit.

Pete had a house and that's where I would go with Ben, always saying I was going to the clinic. I had a lot more freedom when it was caravan season and Mum was away, and I always found out what Dad would be doing that day.

'Busy day?' I'd ask over breakfast.

'Contractors on site from first thing until God knows when,' he might say, and that would be my ticket to time with Pete that day. Although he worked in a garage, he always managed to slip away or ring in sick – it didn't really matter as it was a cash-in-hand job anyway. Those times were my escape. When Mum wasn't there, it was horrific with Dad – he had us living like a married couple. I'd go to bed when I put Ben in his cot in the evening and Dad would come into my bed for the whole night. He was still raping me four nights a week, it never went above that for some reason, but it certainly never dropped either; it was as if he was working to his own timetable. I'd make his dinner for when he came home, do his washing, make sure the house was clean. If he ever felt poorly, I was expected to nurse him with cups of tea and cold flannels if he had a migraine. Then, if it was one of his nights, he'd abuse me.

I was his wife in all but name.

And with Pete? Well, with Pete it couldn't have been more different. I cried the first time we had sex. I didn't know such an act could actually be nice – it felt right and he was so caring.

'Have I hurt you, Mandy?' he asked, looking worried.

'No, no, really I'm OK, it was just lovely.'

It hadn't been nice with my previous boyfriends, it had just been something to do, whereas Pete had waited and he made it as much about how I felt as it was about him. That he was concerned he had hurt me just blew me away. Even ordinary things like kissing and having gentle moments were a whole new world to me.

Pete was great with Ben, more attentive than I was. Any time I managed to get away into town to meet him, the baby would be with me. Pete would pick him up and play with him, and he even took him into a photo booth one day to get pictures taken of them both. I took the strip of photos and stuck them in my wardrobe behind my clothes. Mum found them and ripped them all up, but I remember how lovely they were.

Ben used to go to a child development clinic at the hospital on Mondays. It was a group for kids with special needs, a playgroup with special exercises. Each little one needed a key worker and I was allocated a woman called Carol Jones. Pete and I would sometimes meet at the clinic with Ben if Dad wasn't coming, as it was one of the only places we could be together apart from Pete's house.

My gram had moved to a flat nearby and it looked on to the clinic – she had accepted things a bit more by now, although our relationship wasn't anywhere near as close as it had been when I was little. Deep down, I could never forgive her for telling me to deny that I'd been abused. I took what I could get though, I took the dregs as I thought so little of myself. I can only assume that Mum had been there one day and saw Pete go in with me because she strolled in as if she owned the place, came up to me and spat in my face. Without a word, she walked out.

'You're nothing but a P*ki slag, are you? Wait till your dad finds out, he'll go mad,' she told me when I got back.

She was right and he hit the roof, while she sat there smiling, delighted that she'd engineered it all.

'What are you doing, hanging around with that sort? You'll get a name for yourself!' he roared.

I couldn't have cared less, but it was now out in the open that she – and therefore my dad – knew about Pete.

* * *

'I'm going to tell people,' Pete said one day out of nowhere, the upset clear in his voice.

'You're going to tell them what?'

'That your dad has sex with you – he does, doesn't he?' he asked.

I need to stop here for a moment (again!) because I don't think that paints Pete in a very good light, but it also shows just how much the language around abuse matters. Until I wrote this book, as I've said, I never even used the word 'rape' for what my father did. If you've never had any experience of the horrific way men abuse children, you might not realise how big this change in language is. And let me say at this point, I've no time for 'whataboutery' – don't tell me women sexually abuse children too because that's such a ridiculously small number compared to what men do. Of course they sometimes do it, or they facilitate men doing it, and of course they emotionally, physically and psychologically abuse (as my own mother did), but there's no epidemic of women out there, raping children. Back then, you'd hear people talking about 'perverts' or 'kiddie-fiddlers', but the words are rape and paedophilia. When Pete spoke about 'sex', he had no idea how that minimises what's being done to a child, how it makes it seem so much less appalling than it actually is. But I can't blame him for that, given that I wasn't even using the right words either.

All I said in reply was 'Yeah.'

'He's weird. That man is weird, I've always known. Is he Ben's dad?'

What could I say other than 'I don't know'? I was 99 per cent sure but there was no way I wanted to verbalise that to another person, even someone I had allowed to get close. Once it was out there, I couldn't be in denial any longer.

I've dissociated with this a bit – Pete knew that I was being abused by my father, but I can't remember how he worked it out or when he realised. I know it was round about this time but I can't be more specific. It would be so much easier for stories to have neat timelines, wouldn't it? Life doesn't work that way. Everyone's memory is messy but when you add trauma and extreme coping mechanisms into the mix, it would be a complete lie for me to sit there and write, 'This happened in May that year, then three days later this happened before there was a break of 17 days and three hours before the next thing.' It's not just unlikely that would happen in a mind that was being broken like mine, it would also be a downright lie. I'm trying to be 100 per cent honest with what I'm telling you, but I know there will be people out there who will read this and say, 'She doesn't remember when her boyfriend first knew her dad was raping her?' They'll roll their eyes and think I must be a liar. You know what? Let them think that, because anyone who is a survivor of any type of abuse will recognise what I'm saying – they'll see themselves in these words and they'll understand fully that our minds do what they can to protect us, in whatever tiny or huge ways possible, because we've been ripped apart by so many other things.

No, I don't remember when Pete knew or how he found out – but he did. Dad always seemed to be with me, he rarely let me go out. If I went shopping, he'd be looking out the window for as long as I was in sight.

'What a bastard your dad is and what a bastard thing he's been doing to you all these years! I'm going to tell someone one day, Mandy, I swear I am.'

Dear Mandy

You can do this. It might not seem as if you can, but your strength is building. You might not think you are a good mother, but your love is building too. You've had no role model of how to be a good mother, how to be a caring parent, and I know that you feel you aren't doing this properly, that you don't feel what you think you *should* feel. Any time your thoughts go there, I wish I could tell you to remind yourself of all you've done so far.

You've endured all of this to protect others – your sisters, now your son. You have put your own pain and your own horror to one side and done more than could ever have been asked of you. Mandy, I know that you're fighting for Ben more than you are for yourself, but you're a team, you *are* a family. If you get out, *when* you get out, it will be for all of you. There's a future there with Pete if you can both just hold on. It might seem as if the world is against you (and why wouldn't you think that after everything you've experienced?), but there is fire in you that your father has never been able to put out.

You know how to get through anything.

You know how to wait and find your moment.

You know that there will come a moment when the life you deserve will be there for you.

Hold on, Mandy, hold on.

9

Telling

Although I was an adult, I was so childlike, very naïve and timid – I'd never lived. I'd never been to a club, never been on holiday with friends, I'd never been allowed to do daft stuff so that I could learn from it. I was just in whatever role Dad wanted me to be in, I was his toy.

By that point I was sleeping on the couch as my room was damp and Ben kept getting chest infections. Dad would rape me there with my baby next to me. His bedroom with Mum was closer than ever, right next to the living room, but it seemed she couldn't care less.

I never really chose to cuddle Ben – I would feed him or rock him if he cried, but I was never consumed with love.

Mum would say, 'Oh, I could eat you!' to him and lots of rubbish like that, but it sickened me how she spoke to him and I certainly never felt that way. I could look back on those times when I wasn't connected to Ben with sadness, but they're in the past and I know how I feel about him now. There's no point dwelling on it – Ben won't benefit but it's taken me a while to get to that place of acceptance. I know I was finding a way to cope, a way to get through the enormous trauma I'd suffered even if I didn't label it that way back then. It was obvious that Ben's problems were getting worse and I could see other kids developing so much quicker. Although he was a year and half now, he still wasn't walking, he wasn't talking, he was barely crawling. He was given monthly checks for his heart and the child development people were very good at giving me exercises to try and make him get a little better, but as it had been from the start, Mum and Dad just didn't encourage him, they wanted him to stay dependent – it didn't bother them. I'd always thought Ben's problems were because of him being Dad's son but that wasn't something I could ever say to him.

I did wonder how my parents managed to just keep going as if everything was perfectly normal, but somehow they did and we would have trips to the caravan just as we'd always done. I'd lie there in the tiny excuse for a bed, listening to Dad's snores and knowing that the clinking noise was Mum shuffling about feet away, pouring herself a drink. That caravan was like some hideous metaphor for our existence – all of us shoved into a tiny space, cramped together, forced to pretend to the outside world that we were such a happy, loving family that we even went on holiday together – but there was one time when Mum went there on her own with my sisters and I was back to being raped whenever he felt like it. With an empty house, he could do whatever he wanted without even putting on a pretence of being careful.

That night though, something felt different. When he got into bed beside me, I pushed him away.

'No, not tonight,' I told him. 'You're a pig! Get away from me.'

He pushed me out of the bed and got up. The room had wooden framed doors with stained glass in them and he slammed the door so hard, the glass smashed. 'That's your fault! Look what you made me do – clean it up!' he shouted. I did as I was told but my mind kept spinning. Yes, he'd smashed the door, but he'd done nothing else. I'd never said anything like that to him before and I felt tremendous, immediate guilt that it was so easy. If he didn't keep going just with me saying that, why hadn't I said something before? I thought about it all night and wondered if maybe I was stronger than I'd realised.

As soon as it was light, I got up. He was already in the kitchen.

'I want to leave home,' I told him without any preamble.

'What are you talking about? Why would you want to do that?' he asked.

'I've got a child now, Dad – it's time to move out. Friends

have done that, it's just what happens.'

He stared at me with cold, cold eyes. 'If you leave this house, you go out as you came into the world – with nothing.'

'Fine.'

'I mean it, Mandy. Get your clothes off if you're going. Now! And take the baby's clothes off too.'

'Are you kidding me?' I asked.

'Do I look like a man having a laugh?' he sneered. 'Do it! Make the choice. Stay and shut up, or take every last stitch off and get out.'

'Easy choice,' I said, starting to peel my clothes off. It took just seconds and I moved towards the door, thinking he would at least throw something at me so that I could cover up. When he didn't, I looked out onto the street and thought to myself, *dear God, I could actually do this*. There were no cars about, it was still early, but I didn't have a stitch on and someone could see me at any moment – actually, that would have been OK as I would have got in anyone's car to get away from there. I held Ben to me, both of us naked and shivering, but just as I got to the end of the drive, I heard him behind me.

'Get back in here, you stupid bitch!' he snarled, slapping the side of my head. 'Where are you going to go? You can't even look after your kid properly, how do you think you'd survive?'

So, I got Ben dressed, got myself dressed as Dad got

himself ready for work as if it was just another normal morning. Broken, beaten down, I resigned myself to the fact I'd failed. What was the point in me even trying?

* * *

When I missed a couple of periods in March 1988, I was desperate for the baby to be Pete's if I did turn out to be having another one. I told him that I thought I was pregnant and arranged to meet him at the chemist, where they would do an over-the-counter test, where you went back after an hour to get the results.

'I'm taking Ben out to get some food!' I shouted as I went out the door, trying not to hang around and get questioned. Instead of paying board at home, I bought everything Ben needed to eat, which meant that my parents were used to me popping out for bits for him, but Mum was right there that day as I went down the path.

'He doesn't need anything, we've got plenty in,' she said, eyeing me suspiciously. 'Are you up to something?'

'I've told you, I'm just getting a few bits for him.'

'I'll come with you. Hold on while I get ready,' she said, turning around.

'No, no, I need to get out. I'll take him for a walk in the pram too,' I told her, but I could see her watching me as I went down the street.

I met Pete outside the chemist, did the test and then we went for a wander until it was time to go back.

'We've already given the test results to your mum,' the counter assistant told me when we returned.

'What do you mean? Why would you do that?'

'She came in and said you couldn't make it back, so we told her.'

That was all kinds of ridiculous but all I could think was that Mum had followed us to the pharmacy after her suspicions had been raised.

'Anyway,' she added, 'it's positive: you're pregnant.'

I was so shocked that they had given my mother the results that I barely took in that they were telling me I was pregnant again. But I was. My parents knew before I did and when I got back, it all kicked off instantly.

'You slag!' Mum yelled as soon as I got in the door. 'I hear you're pregnant. Well, you're not having it, just wait till your dad hears this. There's no way you're having a P*ki baby!' And she kept ranting: 'I don't see how you've got pregnant again, Mandy. Once is understandable but not twice! You're an absolute state, you know that?'

'You'll have to get rid of it,' Dad chimed in after work when she told him. He must have been certain this time it wasn't his or he wouldn't have said that. 'You'd never be able to cope, what with Ben and his needs.'

'Ben will be 18 months when I have it – you don't know what he'll be like by then,' I said.

'He's not going to magically get better, is he? No, Mandy, you don't get a say in this. You're getting rid of it.'

I genuinely believed the baby was Pete's but I also knew that I had no choice. If Mum and Dad had decided I was getting an abortion, then that's what would happen – I wasn't strong enough to fight them.

Pete and I could only meet when I arranged it and when we did finally manage to see each other, he said, 'It's up to you, Mandy – I'll support you whatever you decide.'

I was only about eight weeks gone when I got the results, but I desperately wanted a baby with Pete and I'd convinced myself that it was his, so any talk about an abortion was awful. But Mum set up all the appointments and I went along with it. I remember my GP calling at one point and asking me if I was sure: 'You don't have to go ahead with this, Mandy – not if you don't want to.'

'I do, I do have to go ahead with it,' I told him.

I was still only 21 at this point and had no control over my life whatsoever – I wasn't even allowed to make decisions for myself.

Carol, the social worker I knew from Ben's clinic appointments, was around quite a bit at this time and so I asked her if she could help arrange the abortion. I had no idea she was about to become such a big part of my life.

On the day itself, I was in a waiting room with lots of other women. Dad took me and sat with me the whole time and I felt the nurses treated me really badly. When one of the women asked what I was there for, I just said 'an abortion' as I had no idea that there was a stigma attached to it in some people's minds. No one spoke to me after that.

I must have blocked out a lot as the next thing I remember is going home. There's nothing else, just me in the car with Dad taking me home. I don't remember the operation, I don't remember any follow-up checks and I don't remember a lot of even being there – I guess I dissociated with that too, I've put it all away in the box where I keep things. I don't know if I had any sense of sadness about the baby as I didn't know whether it was Pete's for sure, and I never will know, but it was just something to get through. I certainly don't feel that there's a child missing in my life now as it could have been Dad's.

He gave me a rest for a week before he started raping me again.

'You need to keep away from that P*ki,' he kept saying. 'Don't go near him, do you hear me?'

'I don't see him any more now,' I lied. 'It's over.'

'Good – you know we're going to run away together one day, don't you, Mandy? You can't be seeing anyone else because it's going to be just us soon.'

He went back to that a lot.

'Would you ever run away with me?'

'Do you think we'll be happy when we run away?'

'Will you run away with me one day, Mandy?'

Sometimes I told him no, but most of the time he didn't need me to say anything – he was just verbalising some sick old fantasy in his head that we were a couple and we just needed to find the strength to escape and have some sort of wonderful life together with Ben as a family. As I was getting older, although I still found him disgusting, I also blamed myself for being part of it. *There must be something wrong with me*, I thought. *This isn't happening to everyone so what have I done to bring it about?* It had been going on for almost a decade by now and I just couldn't understand why he would want to do *that* and the only reason I could come up with was that it was my fault. I admit that when I was little – before it began – I did love my dad, but I'd hated him for years now.

If he'd been caught when I was 11, he would have been recognised as a paedophile. Now that I was an adult woman, if it was common knowledge then I'd be blamed too – I knew that. He'd been raping me as a child and as a woman, so did that mean it was just me, it was whatever age I was, so *I* was the issue? In some ways, it didn't matter, did it? I'd always had to protect my sisters and if I allowed him to rape me, he would hopefully keep away from them, that was still my mindset.

Pete and I hadn't seen each other while all this was going on, but after the abortion, I met him in town with Ben one day. I didn't mind going into town, I didn't feel people were talking about me as no one knew me anyway – I was pretty much always at home, there was no chance I was going to bump into anyone or be their topic of conversation.

'You need to leave, Mandy, you really do. Look at what they're doing to you. I know he's been abusing you for years, but now, the abortion – it won't stop, you must be able to see that?' Pete told me.

'I know, I know, but I can't leave. I'll go to prison, no one will believe me if I tell, they all think he's such a great man and they threw me in a cell the last time. They'll do it again,' I said.

'You won't!' he insisted.

'I will, he has that power.'

Sadly, Pete just couldn't cope with it all. 'This is killing me, I can't deal with it anymore. You know I love you, Mandy, but it just doesn't look like we can ever be together while he's around,' he told me.

Two days later, I was putting the washing away when Mum came into the kitchen.

'You all right, Mandy?' she asked, which was unusual.

'I'm fine,' I said as I always did.

She turned to leave and then muttered, 'Oh, by the way, that P*ki's dead. He killed himself.' She started laughing. 'That's what happens when people have anything to do with you, you're poison.'

I believed her, I really did. Sitting on the floor crying, all I could think was that Pete had loved me and now he was gone – any hope had gone with him too.

The next day, I went round to his house, which was all locked up. There was a lad walking up the street and I asked him to kick the door in as I needed to see for myself what had happened, I had to know for sure that Pete was gone. There was blood everywhere, the place was wrecked, and when I saw that I felt as if a little something else inside me had died. Pete had believed in me, he'd tried to help me, he'd encouraged me to get out and it hadn't worked. Maybe Mum was right, maybe I *was* poison. I decided to go to Pete's sister's house to see if I could find out any more about what had happened. She opened the door to me and before I'd had the chance to ask her anything, she said, 'I think you'd better come in.'

Pete was sitting there. He'd cut his face and neck, and had bandages all over his wrists. He hadn't tried to kill himself, he'd self-harmed but not meant to take it as far as he did. All I could think was, *you're here, you're here – you haven't gone, you're still here!*

Before I could speak, Pete came over to me, grabbed my hands and said, 'I did this because of what's happening to you, Mandy – I just can't stop it, can I? I can't protect you so what's the use of me?'

'You know I can't leave, I've told you a hundred times. I can't just up and go,' I said sadly.

'Will you ever?' he asked.

'I don't know, I honestly don't know,' I admitted.

'Do you want something to change, or do you want this to be your life?'

'I don't want it! How could I want this?'

'Then you have to think about what has to happen, Mandy – you can't go on like this but neither can I,' he told me.

I went back home, not knowing what else there was for either of us to say, but it became a turning point: Pete's accident was the impetus for him to tell the health visitor, who he knew from Ben's clinic.

She came up to our house, which she'd never done before.

'What are you doing here?' I asked, just grateful that no one else was in.

'I need to speak to you. The boy you come to clinic with has called in and made an allegation about your dad and I need to know if it's true. Is your dad abusing you, Mandy?'

Quick as a flash, I said, 'We've fallen out, he's just doing it to spite me.'

'Are you sure?'

'Yes, definitely.'

'Thank God for that!'

And that was that. In a flash, everything Pete had been brave enough to say was dismissed.

Soon afterwards Pete moved to Blackpool and I didn't see him again until December 1988, seven months after the abortion. My life went back to being utter shit during that time – staying in that house, being told I was a useless mother and a compete slag, having Dad do what he wanted to me those four nights a week and all the while my mum chose to ignore it. It was as if the only hopeful chapter in my life had closed.

I was friendly with the daughter of a couple who owned the local fish and chip shop. I was allowed to go and meet her because I worked for them part-time and I knew when Pete came back so I asked him if he would meet me there. He walked me home that night and we just fell straight back into the conversations we'd always had, with him asking me to leave and me telling him it just couldn't happen. Even if I had the strength to get out, I wouldn't leave my little boy.

'I need to go back, Pete, I always need to go back,' I said.

'You need to leave,' he tried to reason with me. 'That disgusting bastard can't keep doing this to you.'

'You know I can't leave Ben, you know that,' I said, furious that he would ever think I could.

I went to push him and as I did so, I scratched his face with my long nails. Without meaning to, as a jerk reaction, he pushed me back and I hit my head against the wall. Blood running down my face, I ran home. It was just after midnight and Dad was still waiting up for me. As soon as he saw me, he said, 'I bet I know who did that to you! It was that P*ki, wasn't it?'

'I don't want to talk about it!' I cried.

'That's fine. I'm calling the police, let's see what they say.'

They were there almost instantly, which wasn't surprising given that they knew Dad and they were all great pals.

'What happened?' one of them asked me.

'Pete pushed me, I'm fine.'

'You need stitches,' Dad decided.

'He punched you?' asked the copper.

'No! That's not what I said. He pushed me because I was laying into him.'

'He punched you, I think,' said Dad.

'I think you're right, Keith,' the copper replied. 'That's not on, is it? Punching a young lass?'

Pete was arrested, fined and bailed for common assault, which meant that he wasn't allowed near me for another year. He left again for Blackpool where his mum lived and any hope of me having something, someone, for myself again was taken away – but not before he kept to his word and told someone else just what he had suspected all along.

I got a call from a health visitor called Marjorie one day, completely out of the blue.

'Can you come into the clinic for a quick chat, Mandy?' she asked.

'About what?' I said, immediately suspicious as Ben didn't have any scheduled appointments.

'Oh, nothing to worry about, but can you pop in this morning?' she said, breezily.

So, I got Ben ready and went to the clinic, which was in the centre where he was always checked. When I got there, Marjorie was pacing up and down in the reception.

'You're here! Fantastic – let's find somewhere to talk.'

She took me into a meeting room and asked me to sit down. 'I've had a call, Mandy,' she began. 'Some lad ... Well, he's made some very serious allegations.'

'About what?' I said.

'It's hard to know how to even say this but he's told me some terrible things. He says your father's been abusing you and it's been going on for years.'

I took a deep breath; I didn't want this, I didn't want Pete to have said anything and I didn't want to risk anyone investigating because they might take Ben off me, they might even put me in jail. I didn't think for one second that they would do anything to punish Dad – I just assumed that he would get away with everything as he always did.

'Oh, I know what this is about,' I replied. 'It'll be Pete. He was a lad I was seeing, but we've broken up now.'

Marjorie was visibly relieved. 'So, he's just making trouble?'

'Absolutely.'

'Not a shred of truth in it?' she persisted and I swear if she could have crossed her fingers to hope for my answer being the one she wanted, she would.

'No, none at all.'

'Fantastic! I thought as much – what a thing for him to

say! Well, that's all I need from you, Mandy – would you like a lift home?'

And that was that. Marjorie didn't mention a word of the allegation on the drive back and it was never brought up again by anyone. Years later, when I was to get my scant records, this 'incident' would be referred to as 'the second disclosure'. But it was barely that – it never came from me and no one ever scratched beneath the surface of what Pete had said anyway.

He'd tried – and I had said 'no' yet again.

10

Leaving

It was obvious what would happen next, wasn't it? I fell pregnant again. It was the spring of 1989 and I hadn't had sex with Pete so there was no doubt at all this time. It was seven months before I got this one confirmed – I knew I was having a baby, I knew it was Dad's and I told no one. I planned to give birth and leave the child somewhere and for that, I had to keep it a secret. I'd wrap the baby up and probably leave it in the Botanic Gardens, where someone would find it and keep it safe, and that was honestly what I thought was the best plan for me and the little one. I was tiny anyway – did Dad notice anything when he was raping me? He didn't say, but I doubt it would have mattered. He didn't care either way, did he?

I had no healthcare or tests, no input from the community midwife team and when my mum and dad finally noticed, I was sent for a scan.

The first thing the sonographer said to me after looking at my notes and before he put the jelly on me was, 'I see your first son's a retard, isn't he? You'll be worried about this one.'

I couldn't even think what to say and Mum, at my side, said nothing either.

The baby was too big for the scan photo as I was eight months gone.

'We'd best get some baby stuff,' was all she muttered as we went home before adding, 'Christ, Mandy, imagine you letting this happen again!'

After she'd told Dad it was confirmed, there was a difference in him – the only way I can describe it was that he was shitting himself. He came into my room that night but didn't lie down beside me. Instead, pacing the floor, he whispered, 'What if they do blood tests, Mandy? What if they find out? Jesus, I can't have this, I can't have them checking!'

It was the only time I'd ever seen him panic to that degree. He didn't let it go and the next day, in his caretaker's office at school, he went back to it again: 'They'll do blood tests because you're so far on. They won't understand why you didn't go to the doctor earlier, they'll start asking questions and they'll do tests. What will I do, Mandy, what will I do?'

There were no signs of panic when Mum walked in on him raping me, but this was really freaking him out.

Of course, my plans of giving birth alone and leaving the

baby somewhere had gone now that my parents were fully aware of what was happening. This one was Dad's too, I knew that for a fact, which meant it was likely to be disabled as well. How could I cope with that? After a few days, they were both delighted (Dad never expressed his concerns again at that point), just as they had been with Ben, and it wasn't long before I gave birth, a couple of weeks early.

As soon as I had my second little boy, Calvin, I could see he was different to Ben. He wasn't floppy, there were no obvious signs that he was anything but 'normal'. It was hard to believe he was perfect given that I knew he was my father's child, born of rape. But like Ben, I felt nothing for him – in fact, even more so because of not being in any doubt and also not even feeling sorry for him having to cope with all the things my first son was afflicted with. I know that makes me seem the most horrible person – the most awful mother you could imagine – but it was a combination of so many things, so many years of abuse, and the feeling I'd had after Ben that I would just be a production line of kids now. People will judge, I know that, but I know there are other women who on reading this will be relieved to find that they're not alone in their feelings if they've been there. I had no doubt of who the father was, I had full knowledge of what happened in my bed four times a week, and I also think that I was deliberately distancing myself from this new baby as I needed to be strong. I couldn't crumble or I'd be no use to anyone. I'd never harm a hair on his head, but my God, it was hard to go on.

After the birth I had some retained placenta and needed a blood transfusion, which meant that I had to stay in hospital and my parents were there constantly. But they didn't focus on Calvin as much as they had with Ben and it meant that when I got home, I had more time with him. I was still being told I was useless though and I believed it as I didn't have any sort of maternal rush for my new baby. It was just the same as it had been with Ben.

After having Calvin, I felt that was my life – I would have baby after baby to my father. I feel in my heart that he would have accepted them disabled, struggling, even dead, because it would mean that he still controlled me. Ben had been diagnosed with cerebral palsy but I couldn't help wondering where exactly all his problems had come from – I didn't really understand about the ramifications of incest but I knew it was the root cause. Keith Meadows had dripped poison into me and Ben had paid a price beyond anything that could be imagined.

Dad treated Calvin differently immediately. He always called him by his name, never 'son'. This time he was much more in the role of grandfather because he was so focused on Ben, his firstborn son. The blood transfusion at least gave me some respite from him raping me for two or three weeks – wasn't I lucky?

Now with two kids, did I have a hope that things might

be different? Maybe, but I was looked on as a childminder – I was never allowed to take both my children out at the same time and I was back to being treated like an idiot.

'Don't be stupid, you can't cope with both of them,' Mum would tell me. 'You're useless even when you're sat at home, how would you manage?'

'If we got a double buggy, I could,' I told her. If I had both my boys in one of those, I would be able to get out and just walk for miles every day.

'And how are we going to afford that? We're not millionaires, Mandy – and now we've got even more mouths to feed!'

Like everything else, my parents took over. I'd get to be at home alone with Calvin whenever they took Ben to hospital appointments so it gave me more of an opportunity to play with him and be a mum, certainly more than I'd done with Ben. But I still never truly engaged. My time with Calvin gave me some realisation that things weren't changing, I wasn't miraculously turning into some perfect mother in the sense that I thought a perfect mother *should* be, I was just Mandy – still a very young woman who was living a nightmare. In all honesty, I don't know whether I could have been any different. I was a product of what had been done to me and my sons were too. It was madness to think it could ever have been 'normal' and all I could hold on to was that I did feel a fierce protectiveness for them and I hoped that would be enough.

My parents were so soft with Ben – they picked him up, carried him, fed him, they never pushed him into achieving more, they never encouraged him – and I think that's affected him to this day. If he'd been treated as the boy he could have been rather than the dependent child they wanted him to be, who knows what he might have achieved? I don't think he recognised me as his mother at all. They were his world because they made sure that would be the case. Sometimes I would watch them with him and not recognise the people I saw in front of me. This was a man who had raped me since I was 11, this was a woman who had witnessed it and told him he had nothing to be sorry for, yet they were picture-perfect grandparents. That's sick really, isn't it? It shows they had that ability, that capacity to love and care – they just chose never to use it for me.

I went through all of the motions of being a mum to Calvin but it was hard, like there was a block. The only time I think I ever let it break through was one day when Gloria from the chip shop came to visit. I was sobbing when she came in and she asked if I had postnatal depression.

'I don't know,' I told her. 'What's that?'

'Probably the baby blues – women just get a bit low after having babies sometimes,' she told me as I wept uncontrollably. 'It'll pass.'

But it didn't feel like it ever would. I felt like I was stuck there forever, two kids and the cold realisation that no one was coming to save me. Calvin seemed healthy enough and, for me, I would never have been able to even contemplate getting away with two babies who had special needs so I still felt trapped: two children was such a bigger deal, such a bigger commitment. I'd been having some thoughts about escaping from the moment I met Pete, hoping that I would be with him forever, no matter what life threw at us. He was the first person who had ever said to me, 'I know.' It wasn't just that I loved him, but that he loved me despite what had been done to me, whereas I always thought I'd be judged – but now? Not just a mum of two, but a woman who had two children by her own father.

Pete had come back as there were some family issues for him to deal with. I told him that Calvin was the baby of someone I'd had a short relationship with and he seemed to accept that; I also said that I wasn't still seeing this imaginary bloke. It was hard not to be with Pete but it was just something else to accept, hoping that one day we'd find a way to be together. Fate would surely work her magic – but I also had dark thoughts about the fact that Dad would also hopefully die at some point and I'd be free of him. It was my only way out. Him dying would be the best option because that would mean I wouldn't be the one who was punished, because now I wondered whether I would be the one who would go to prison if I reported him. They chucked me in a cell once, what was to stop them doing it again? My dad would never admit to raping me when I was a child and everyone would believe him anyway as he was such a nice guy. This was compounded by how he was with Ben. Everyone saw that he had a daughter who'd had a baby outside of marriage and there he was, looking after the poor disabled soul. To top it off, she'd gone and had *another* baby, no shame at all, and good old Keith was providing for them all. What a saint!

I had to have both of my babies christened at The Salvation Army, but with Calvin, there was a different minister doing the service and he refused to do it in front of the congregation because I was sinful. I had to have him christened on a Friday with no one else from the normal attendees there. Hardly a celebration. So I stood with the Major while Calvin was in my arms, in front of a wooden bench with a red cloth on it. I committed my son to a life as a soldier in The Army, marching for God, and barely remember anything else from that day. Throughout the whole thing, I zoned out: it was just something else to get through, another performance to make my father seem like a good man. I did as I was told at every step – I was a zombie, a member of the walking dead – but I'd never let him see how much I was hurting. Of course, it was different when I was alone and I'd sob my heart out, thinking this was how my life was going to be – maybe forever, because what if I died before Dad? I'd never get to be with Pete, I'd never know happiness.

Until I decided I could.

11

This is It

Honestly, it was a spur-of-the-moment decision and I can't believe I ever found the strength. Calvin was seven months old when I left. I phoned Pete on an impulse and just said, 'Meet me at the park.' As soon as I saw him, I told him that I was leaving.

'I've had enough, I can't do it any longer.'

Holding me in his arms, Pete whispered, 'I'm coming with you, we'll do this together. I'll go back to work and finish things off there then see you at the train station.'

'I'll grab some stuff for Calvin. I can do this, Pete, I know I can,' I said.

I went back and took just baby milk, nappies and a pair of knickers for me. My sister had taken Ben out, but I swore I would come back for him. He had an appointment in a few days' time for grommets, which meant that he had to stay until that was over anyway. But I was petrified – I did things so quickly, almost as if I was being chased, because someone could come in at any point and catch me. I put everything in the bottom of the pram and just ran.

Pete turned up at the train station not long after I got there. 'Are you sure about this, Mandy?' he asked.

'Absolutely.'

'It's getting late – why don't we just stay somewhere for the night so that we're not dragging Calvin about and then leave in the morning? Where are we going anyway?'

'The first train that comes in,' I told him.

We found a cheap B&B, signed in under a random name and made our way wearily up to the room. I knew that once Mum and Dad realised that I wasn't coming back that night, they'd go to the police and report me missing. All night, as we lay there with Calvin lying between us, I was petrified that the door would be knocked in and my dad would be there. He would kill me if he found me, I was sure of it. Then my mind flitted back to Ben: was I wrong not to have taken him too? What about his hospital appointment? To me, that mattered more – I'd go back for him once he'd had the operation and I knew that my parents would look after him. At least I thought I could trust them to do that.

'Are you sure about this, Mandy?' Pete kept asking.

'I am – this is one choice I can make and I know it's the right one. I don't know if he'll ever hurt Calvin – I can't take that chance – and I can't stay there any longer to protect my sisters. I have to get out,' I told him firmly.

I had a tiny little notebook with me, which I have to this day. All it says on that date is *MY NEW LIFE 21 AUGUST 1990*.

I actually slept peacefully for the first time in my life. Pete kept asking if I was sure about leaving Ben but I was the one to reassure him that we'd get him back eventually, when the time was right.

'You've done the right thing, Mandy, but it can't stop here – it'll have to go further. He needs to pay for what he's done to you. You'll have to go to the police,' Pete told me.

'Not yet, I can't do that yet. Just let me get this bit over with first, then I'll work out what to do next. That'll be the next hurdle.'

We cuddled all night and it was lovely. In our tiny B&B room with Calvin beside us, everything was peaceful.

The first train in the morning was for Leeds and then we went on to Bridlington, where we stayed in another B&B. My notebook says that we stayed there for two nights then went to Hull before moving on to the William Booth Hostel, a Salvation Army place. In retrospect, I can see this was a foolish move as my dad had contacts in all the 'Sally Ann' places, but we just needed somewhere cheap, clean and safe. *MISSING BEN LOADS*, the notebook says. I think maybe that was the first time I had any maternal feelings for him as I hadn't been away from him for any period of time before. But I shouldn't have been worried – I'd be discovered before I'd even had a chance to make real plans.

We went to Bridlington from Hull on 21 August and the police tracked me down somehow – I think it was through the hostel link when Pete had signed on – and they turned up at the door. I was still wary of saying anything, even though the police were right there and I could have told them why I left, but my parents had Ben and the sheer terror of never getting him back was the biggest thing in my life. The police could see that we were all safe and well so they went on their way, thinking there was nothing for them to follow up on.

'I don't want my mum and dad to know where I am,' I told them.

'They don't have to – we'll just say you and Calvin are fine,' one of the officers assured me.

Now I could breathe. I should have known though: the police might have been keeping their promise but we were in a Salvation Army hostel and someone must have told Dad our whereabouts. We'd had to use our real names as the rent was being partly paid by Social Security – there wouldn't have been any support if we didn't have identification – and I can only guess that my surname was recognised as 'Keith's daughter' and someone, basically, grassed us up.

Pete popped out one night to get chips and no sooner had he left than there was a knock on the door. The woman who was usually on reception was standing there.

'There's someone for you downstairs,' she snapped.

'I don't have time to be going up and down with messages for people, so you'd better deal with it yourself.'

I went down with Calvin in my arms – and there was Dad.

He sighed dramatically. 'Are you coming home then?'

I felt as if he'd punched me in the gut. How, after all this, was he just standing there, as if nothing had happened? It sounds almost unbelievable to admit but they had Ben so I agreed, just like that, just as if it hadn't taken every fibre of strength in my body to get away in the first place. I honestly thought that I'd just wait until Ben had his operation then I'd get him back, but at that moment in time, I thought my safest bet was to go back.

'Get your bag,' he told me. 'Be quick about it.'

So, I ran back upstairs, instantly doing what he said just as I'd always done, grabbed a few things and then got into his car. Pete was still out and in my panicked state, I didn't even leave a note. When he got back, the woman on reception told him what had happened and he later told me that he just crumbled. To return after fifteen minutes or so to find me and the little one gone – not only gone, but back to that hellhole – broke him.

On the drive back, Dad drove like a lunatic. He was bumper-to-bumper in the dark with all the other cars on the road and he didn't say a word to me the whole way. As we went over the Humber Bridge I thought he was going to drive over into the water, it was like we were in a police pursuit.

'Dad! Slow down – you're going to kill us all!' I begged from the back seat, where I tightly held Calvin to me. It didn't matter, it was as if he were in his own world. When we got home, everyone looked at me as if I were a piece of dirt on their shoes. Ben wasn't even there for me to cuddle, he was fast asleep in bed.

'Is no one going to say anything? Are you all going to act as if all of this is normal?' I said furiously.

Just silence. Not a word.

I went up to the room where Ben slept and curled myself in at his side. 'We'll get through this,' I told him. 'This is it, this is the last time they bring me back – I'll get out and I'll get you out too, I promise you that. I've done it once, I'll do it again.' I kissed him on the cheek and went back down to the living room. They'd all gone to bed as if it was a normal night. Creeping into the kitchen to make myself a cup of tea, I saw that a drawer was slightly open, one of those drawers full of bits and pieces that we all have. In among the string and candles and batteries and what must have been 100 other things was a pair of scissors. Bright, shiny silver scissors. Quickly, I grabbed them and stuffed them in my pocket. If Dad came near me, I swore to myself, I'd stab him – and I'd never be anywhere around him without those scissors until I managed to escape again.

Looking back, I'm still furious with myself that I returned but no one really understands the power the abuser has over you unless they have been through it themselves.

The control is terrifying and you truly believe that there is no one in the world who can do what they can do. For years, I had been in an abusive, emotionally and psychologically controlling situation. I had no mum to rely on, I was protecting my sisters, I'd been groomed and controlled – was it any wonder that I found myself dragged back in again?

* * *

The next day, I got up from the sofa where Calvin still slept and went into the kitchen.

'Ben's got a child development appointment today,' Mum said, the first time she'd spoken to me since Dad dragged me back. 'I suppose you won't be interested in that.'

'You'd suppose wrong – I'm coming with you.'

'It's not me that's going, it's your dad.'

I turned the scissors round in my pocket. 'That's fine – I'm going, no matter who else is.'

We met Carol, the social worker, there – she was always at these appointments so that she could report back in the files – and the meeting was in a room full of mats and gym equipment for toddlers. There was a window which you could see into if you were on one side, while the other side just looked perfectly normal – you couldn't tell someone was looking at you. Carol and I stood there, watching Dad play with Ben, and I just knew that something was brewing in my mind. I quite liked Carol at this point – she was the one who had helped with the abortion and I didn't feel she judged me.

Ben was lying on the floor, not really doing anything a two-year-old would do. He was on a blue mat with my dad rolling him about, doing the things I'd done before I left – doing the things a parent would do with their child. My son was just in his nappy so that they could look at his skeletal development and a chill went through me.

That monster was touching my baby's skin.

No!

I'd never seen my father touching him like that before and I couldn't stand it. *Get your grubby hands off*, I thought. *He's mine*. The tears began falling.

Carol said, 'Oh no, what's wrong, love? What's wrong?'

'That man,' I replied, pointing at him. 'That man has been having sex with me for years. Ben's his child.'

It came out, clean and as cold as that.

Stunned, Carol could only say, 'Oh, Mandy.' Somehow she got her thoughts together as I continued to stare, shocked that she wasn't immediately telling me to stop lying.

'Right, we're going to get you sorted,' she promised. 'Don't you worry, I'm going to deal with this. But what about your sisters?'

'They're fine – I was there, I did all of it so that he wouldn't touch them. I think they hate me now, but I did it all for them so he wouldn't go near. It's just me,' I told her.

She put her arms around me but the tears had stopped – I didn't want to give him that power even though he was in another room.

Carol pulled out a notepad and began writing some notes then looked up at me.

'What about Calvin?'

'Yep – him too.'

'Oh, Mandy – I'll have to get in touch with Terry, my boss. I'll let him know and well, the ball will start rolling, I guess. Does Pete know?'

'Pete's always known.'

'How long has this been going on?'

'Since I was 11, I think, but it could have been earlier, I guess – I could have blocked it out.'

She seemed to understand.

'Just go in that room when you're called as if nothing's happened, because I'm scared for you. I'll get things in motion. We'll have to get other people involved here, Mandy, and it could be a long process.'

'That's what I want – I want people to be fully aware of what he did. It's time now, it's time for everyone to know what he is. This is it, isn't it?'

Carol nodded.

It was just a few minutes but it would change everything. I'd always hoped that someone else would notice and save me, but it hadn't happened. Now, I'd finally found my voice and I'd done it. I'd told someone and begun the process –

the long, long process – of saving myself. Until I wrote this, I always thought Pete had saved me but that isn't actually true. That moment of seeing my father touch my little boy's skin is seared onto my memory and it was what pushed me into telling Carol, pushed me into finally speaking out. I've never thought of it like that before now. Maybe Carol had her suspicions – she certainly believed me straight away – but I knew I wouldn't go back on it this time. I'd escaped once, I could do so again and I'd have help now that I had disclosed what had been happening, or at least I hoped this would be the case.

As soon as I went into the room with Dad and Ben, he snapped at me, 'You've been crying, haven't you? What have you got to cry about?'

'Just seeing Ben, you know – seeing what he can't do, I don't like it.'

'Grow up – he's fine!' he snarled.

And that was it, we went home. Did I truly think he would abuse Ben if I didn't do something? I don't know, and not knowing is enough. He might, he might not, but Ben was even more vulnerable – he couldn't talk, he couldn't run away. I might not have felt anything maternal towards him when he was born, but it was a rush of protectiveness that finally gave me my voice that day with Carol. From that moment, Ben was no one else's: he was my boy.

Back home, my mind was whirling as I didn't know what was being done, what conferences were being held, what reports were being written, what was being decided about my future. All I could do was wait, but the hours dragged. As time went on, I began questioning myself. Would they believe me? Would they think that, as a grown woman, I should just move on? Would I get in trouble for even saying those things, for implying that Ben could be at risk if Dad was nearby? I started spiralling downwards – would I ever get out? Would I ever get Ben? Would I ever get justice?

In the early hours of the morning before anyone was up, I stumbled to the kitchen as I'd done the night before when I'd taken the scissors. I now found myself weak and terrified. It was all too much, I should never have told Carol. What if Dad took it out on Ben once he discovered I'd told the truth? Maybe my little boy was actually safer without me. Carol would check up on him if I wasn't around, Dad would be watched. It was as if I was moving in slow motion as I moved towards the cupboard where we kept the medicines. Grabbing the many packets of paracetamol Mum kept for all her aches and pains, I popped them out of their silver foil and shovelled as many as I could down my throat. How could I have been so stupid to think speaking out was the right thing to do? The best thing for everyone would be if I wasn't here. If I stayed, they would probably take both my boys – I'd be without them anyway. It was a mess and it was all my fault.

Almost immediately, I started vomiting and convinced myself that I couldn't do anything properly. I decided

I hadn't taken enough tablets either – I must have been bouncing from side to side as I went to the local shop and bought one of those plastic tubs full of painkillers. I took as many as I could at a time but kept vomiting – they weren't staying down and by the time I got home, all I could do was lie on the floor.

'What's wrong with you?' Mum snapped when she saw me lying on the living-room floor with the tub in my hand. 'Taken tablets, have you? You're a silly bitch, Mandy, always have been, always will be. Looks like you've messed that up too or you'd be dead by now. Desperate for attention, that's all you ever want. Absolutely pathetic. Keith, come and look at this!'

Dad traipsed in. 'What's happening here?'

'Tell her to grow up, Keith – taking tablets, making a show of herself. Look at the state of her!' Mum told him.

'She's not worth talking to,' he said, stepping over me as if I wasn't there.

It was a wake-up call, to be honest. Had it worked, what would have happened to my boys? Almost certainly they would have been left with the loving grandparents, wouldn't they? Even if no one believed me now, I'd tried and I'd keep trying.

Pete had kicked off when he went back to the room at The Salvation Army and found that I'd gone. He'd been moved to a hostel by this point and told that he wasn't entitled to a family room. I rang him there, telling him what I'd said to Carol. I knew that he loved me completely but that it was all taking its toll on his mental wellbeing too – it's hard to think how it wouldn't really. It mattered so much that he'd been the one who'd stood by me, the one who believed me, and he'd gone through so much with it too – it's not easy to love someone like me.

Dad hadn't touched me since I came back, which was a relief given that I was still carrying the scissors everywhere, and I think it was because he believed I was tainted now that I'd been with Pete. But that didn't mean he was going to leave me completely alone.

The day after I'd tried to overdose, he came into the living room while I was sitting on the sofa, Calvin playing at my feet.

'You need cured, Mandy – you need cured,' he said in a weird, low voice.

Cured? It wasn't a word I'd ever heard him use before.

'What are you talking about? What do I need to be cured from?' I asked.

'You're full of sin, you're a liar and you have the stench of the heathen upon you,' he told me.

'You're talking rubbish,' I said firmly, leaning down to move some of Calvin's toy animals about for him. 'This is just your Salvation Army nonsense, isn't it?'

'I'm telling you, you're sinful! You're sinful! You tempted me and you have to be cured!'

He started talking all sorts of nonsense, mumbling stuff

that I couldn't make out. I'd never heard anything like it before in my life.

'God has given me a challenge! That challenge is you, my own daughter! But I WILL cure you, I will save you and get the Devil out of you!'

He ranted on for a bit longer while I just looked at him, my eyes as big as saucers at the display he was putting on, before he ran out of steam. Perhaps a bit disappointed that he hadn't really got the response he might have wanted, Dad just walked away as if nothing had happened and the day continued.

Carol had been in touch to tell me that a case conference had been convened and it would take place about a week after I'd disclosed. There would be police, social workers, all these people discussing me but I wouldn't be allowed to attend even though I was terrified that they'd decide to take the kids away from me. These calls were so hard because Mum and Dad would hover behind me as I spoke on the phone, but Carol would just say, 'Are they there?' If I said, 'Yes' and nothing else, we'd just say our goodbyes and leave it until I could talk.

On the day I knew the case conference was happening, I couldn't settle. By 5 p.m., no one had called me, so I phoned and was told that the boys had been put on the Child Protection Register. Those words sounded terrifying. I asked the woman who had answered the phone what it meant and she just told me that it was to make sure they were safe.

'Are they going into care?'

'No – they're still your responsibility. They're on a register but you won't get any visits or anything like that.'

I don't know if they told my parents but it seemed more of an administrative condition than anything else; no one was actually checking up on me or the boys. So, I kept it all to myself, I carried everything and very quickly, it became too much. I was in regular contact with Pete by that point and we'd met in town one morning without anyone else knowing.

I was quiet for so much of that meeting and he was too. We'd been through a huge amount and yet it felt like I was back where it had started.

'Have you got any money?' I asked him out of nowhere.

'A bit. Not much,' he told me.

'A bit is all we need – we're going for good this time.'

'I'm sorry, Mandy, but I don't believe you – we've been here before.'

'You'll believe me when it happens, Pete – and it will.'

'I can't keep hoping, I can't keep holding on to the promise that we'll be together, away from him. I want to be with you but if it doesn't work this time, I don't think I can do it again.'

'It'll work. This time it will work, I can promise you that. I get my Child Benefit payment on Tuesday, we'll go then.'

I walked back home, knowing that I was going to do it.

On 18 September 1990, I left for the second time, telling my parents that I was going to the Post Office to get my money and do a bit of shopping. The Child Benefit meant freedom to me and I left that house with nothing but Calvin. I took no baby milk or food, nothing that was 'theirs' – and when the two of us walked out, I knew that this time I would only be back to get Ben. I'd held him in my arms before I left, promising that we'd be together soon, knowing that I just had to focus on what I needed to do.

Pete was waiting for me at the train station and as I ran towards him, I thought, *this is it – finally, this is it*. We moved into a bedsit in Chapeltown and I continued to see Carol the social worker. I used to go into Leeds to meet her and she'd take me to Debenhams for something to eat. One day, she said to me, 'Mandy, your mum and dad have applied for Ben to be made a Ward of Court and it's been successful.'

'What does that mean?' I asked her.

Whatever it was, it didn't sound good.

'Well, it means that the High Court becomes his legal guardian and then any decisions about Ben are made through them. It only happens when it's seen that the child has to be safeguarded and protected.'

'Why have they done that?' I wanted to know. 'It's just about control again for them, isn't it?'

'It just means that you wouldn't be able to make decisions about him on big things – he'll still be with your parents in terms of living with them, but legally, they're not his guardians, the High Court is. They've said you're an unfit mum, that you abandoned him – I think you need to get a solicitor, Mandy.'

It turned out that they had lied to their solicitor – who happened to be in The Salvation Army with them – and said that I had agreed to everything. But I wasn't having this: I was going to stand up for what was right and fight for my boy, and for that, I'd need legal representation. Where we lived was a mainly black area and at this time, in Leeds at the turn of the decade, there had been a number of race riots. There were solicitors' offices on every street, with one just across the road from where we lived. I called in and explained my situation to them, asking if they could help.

'Come back at 4 p.m.,' I was told. 'Mark will have a chat and see what he can do for you.'

I was so nervous – I'd had nothing to do with anything like this before – so I went home, picked up a load of washing and went to the launderette, which was next door to the solicitor's office. My mind was spinning in time with the machines as I thought, *I just need to get on with this. It doesn't matter how uncomfortable I am with it all – I need to go into battle for Ben.* I had to get him away from there and I had to get him with me. I'd fight forever to get him back if I had to. I wasn't questioning myself as a mother by this point, something had kicked in once they had got him, once it became official.

No, this is my boy, I said in my mind over and over again. *He's mine and he needs to be with me.*

I trusted Mark straight away.

'You're the first person I've had who has been through this sort of thing, Mandy,' the solicitor told me, 'but I can promise you that I'll help you all I can. We have to contest this. They're saying you support it when you clearly don't. We have to get the case transferred to Leeds from Halifax. I'll deal with Social Services and Carol Jones, then we'll go from there. Can you tell me everything that might be important?'

I had to go through my story again, telling Mark every part of what might 'matter' in the case between my parents and me in the battle for my son. This all happened on 4 October and just over two weeks later, on the 19th, there was another Child Protection Conference at which the police said they were going to press for DNA samples. It was all gathering pace really quickly. It was agreed that 'the police would press their investigations which resulted in hair samples being taken from Keith Meadows, his daughter and the two children as it was suspected that Keith Meadows might be the father of one or both of these children, and these samples were sent for DNA testing.' That was huge.

'Police will come and take you to a surgery in Halifax,' Carol told me. 'They'll take samples from you, Ben and Calvin.'

My reaction was instant: 'I don't want that.'

'Why ever not?' asked Carol.

'They'll hurt him, they'll hurt Ben.'

'No, they won't – it's just a little bit of hair that needs to be taken from the root,' she assured me. 'It'll be over in a second, Mandy, he'll be fine.'

'Do you promise me? I don't want anyone hurting him.'

'I do – I swear it'll be done before he even knows it.'

The police picked me up on the day and, from the moment I set eyes on the detective who was in charge, I knew he didn't like me. I didn't like him either.

'Just do what I say,' he told me. 'If you don't, you'll be facing arrest.'

I had no intention of doing anything wrong, but I just felt he had it in for me given that was the first thing he said. I still had the memory of the first time I'd disclosed in my head, the time I was the one who ended up being thrown in the cells. In the car, from Leeds to Halifax, with Calvin in the car seat, he kept saying over and over, 'You have to do this, you know.'

I did know that everyone expected me to, but I was so unsure. When we got to the GP practice in Halifax, it became too much: 'I'm not doing it,' I told him.

'I've warned you,' he snarled. 'You don't do this, you'll be arrested. Is that what you want?'

'Of course not, but I can't go through with it.'

He rolled his eyes and sighed. 'It's a simple enough

thing. You're not having to do anything, it'll all get done by people who know what's what.'

'No, I can't.'

'Why the hell not?'

'You'll take my kids off me, you'll take them away.'

I took Calvin and walked round for a bit, then went back. The policeman's attitude was still awful and dismissive, like if I didn't go through with it then I was guilty of lying, so I decided to go through with it. I had to jump one way – get arrested or remain terrified that my kids were going to be taken from me.

All of the tests had to be done at the same time so that they couldn't be tampered with and Ben was waiting there with a social worker. I gave him a hug, stroked his head and told him everything would be OK. But I knew he wouldn't understand – maybe I was reassuring myself more than anything.

We were taken into a little room and the doctor did it all very quickly while the police watched. It was just a procedure to them but I felt like I'd done something wrong, as if it was me who was the culprit. I got the sense that they thought I was wasting police time and this was something that didn't matter. The hair samples were put into a little test tube then into evidence bags before they were sent off. Ben was only little, he'd just turned three and had no idea what was going on, but I knew – I knew exactly what they were looking for and I felt disgust radiating off those police officers. Did I imagine it? Maybe, but they could have made things so much easier. Even though Ben had no capacity to know anything, he still had someone pulling his hair out of his head out of nowhere. I was having to deal with normal mum feelings washing over me – out of somewhere had come this avalanche of emotion for him and a desperate need to protect my child. I'll be honest here and say it was weird. I cared for him so much, but it was different to how I feel for my children now who are born from love. Everything I felt for Ben and Calvin now was instinctive though. I would do anything to protect them from harm even if it had been built from someone so twisted.

DNA testing was quite a new technology at that point and the police told me it would take up to a year for the results to come back – and it did take that long. While I waited, there was another wardship case which kept the boys away from me, but the following one saw Calvin returned to me. I went to both of those hearings with Carol, while Pete looked after Calvin. On both occasions, I was kept in a witness room so that no one could see me before I went into court. Their 'side' would be across from us, but Dad wasn't there, he wasn't where I expected him to be. Instead, he was positioned behind me – he was allowed to do that – and I felt his eyes boring into the back of me.

'He never took his eyes off you,' Carol confirmed afterwards. 'He just stared and stared.'

There was nothing in the world that would make me turn around and look at him. He hadn't been charged by that point, so I guess he was still, technically, an innocent man and he could sit where he wanted. And what was Mum doing through all of this? Laughing. She was actually laughing at me. The whole time I kept my eyes on Carol or the floor. I was scared but I wasn't going to buckle and look at him. I felt as if he was commanding me to look at him. I could feel his presence as always and the fear ran through me, but I had to stay strong. Anyone looking at them would have thought they were normal people, dressed smartly, keeping their heads up – but I knew, I knew what they were. In comparison, I must have looked a right scruff. I had nothing to wear but crinkly leggings and an old black top, no doubt looking like the one who was less than reputable against this lovely respectable couple – the respectable couple who had ruined not just my life, but my sons' lives too.

It was such an intimidating environment, a High Court with the judge in his wig and full get-up, someone from the Social Services, everyone there judging me – or at least that's how it felt.

At the second wardship hearing, I left the court with Carol Jones so that we could wait for the decision. The room we were in had half-panelled glass windows and that man, that awful man, stood there staring at me again. Catherine, my solicitor Mark's PA, positioned herself in front of him on our side of the glass, but he kept moving around, trying to see past her, trying to intimidate me with those horrible, evil eyes of his. My team told me it was all a formality and that I should agree to everything and Ben would come back to me eventually; I couldn't really do anything but trust them and follow their advice.

It was still like a dagger to my heart when it was decided that Ben wasn't to come back to me at that point. I was just in a little bedsit in a not-so-nice area, a single mum without much going for her, while they were telling everyone I was unstable, Pete couldn't be relied on, I had taken overdoses, I didn't know how to look after a baby – they won Ben for the time being but I got to keep Calvin.

Mark was saying the same things over and over again, 'This is just what we have to do, Mandy – we're jumping through their hoops, but it will work, you just have to hold on to that. Eventually, Ben will be taken from your parents, he'll go into foster care and that's when you'll be a step closer to getting him back. Don't worry.'

'But I *am* worried!' I said. 'I don't want my baby with them.'

'He's on the At Risk Register, social workers are involved, they're keeping an eye on him – nobody can hurt him. You've made your allegations, the DNA test will come back.'

That didn't comfort me. If a child is being abused, it doesn't matter if social workers are coming in for 10 minutes a week to see if the house is tidy, but I still had to agree to it all or I'd have no chance of ever getting him back.

I can't count how many times I asked Mark, 'Are you sure Ben's safe?' He'd just say that he was but I guess it's just a job to them, isn't it? I don't mean that my solicitor didn't care, but it wasn't his child who was living with people like my parents. Mark did believe me from the start that Dad was the father of Ben though.

Two days after the second court hearing, Calvin went into foster care. The reports say that was 'for the purpose of respite for his mother'. A lot of this was due to Mum. She had found out my address and turned up where I lived. My flat was above a shop and she'd threaten them with violence, saying she'd smash the place up if they didn't let her upstairs to where I was staying and so they felt they had no choice. She was usually drunk when she headed up to Leeds to kick off and the police would usually get called. When she started all her nonsense with the woman who owned the shop, her son would come up to me and say his mother was calling 999 but to be ready for Mum storming up. I'd hear her ranting and raving, calling me all sorts of names downstairs to anyone who would listen, and all I could do was wait for them to arrive.

I have a letter from my files, dated December 1990, which says:

We understand from our client that […] your client Jennifer Meadows went to our client's property without invitation. She attempted to obtain the keys to our client's flat from the landlord and when he refused to release them, she became extremely threatening and abusive.

We understand that when your client was refused the keys to the property, she began hammering on the door and kicking at the door in an attempt to gain entry. The landlord was so concerned as to the nature of the threats made both to himself and our client that he immediately telephoned the police. When your client was informed of this fact she pretended to leave the premises. In fact, she was hiding in the garden and began to hammer on the door as soon as the landlord left. As soon as he became aware of this, he immediately returned and then your client left.

We are very concerned at your client's behaviour, which we consider to be intimidating and threatening in the extreme. We should be obliged if you would speak to your client as a matter of urgency to ask them not to visit our client or attempt to communicate with her in any way save through ourselves.

Mum knew what she was doing even though she was drunk and there is no doubt in my mind that she would have hurt me, given half the chance. There were three reasons for

Calvin going into foster care – the threats from Mum, the fact that the accommodation was seen as unsuitable and no Social Services being available over Christmas. It was only to be for two weeks and I would get him back after Christmas. I remember feeling oddly glad that he was going as I genuinely thought she would get in and hurt both of us – it was all so horrible and I didn't want my boys to see it.

But I was terrified now she had my address and I kept Carol up to date with it all.

'Right, we'll get you moved,' said Carol.

She was true to her word, getting us relocated to a proper house in a posh area. A lovely maisonette in Yeadon, near Bradford Airport, it had two bedrooms for us and the boys when I finally got them home. It was in a crescent of houses at the top of the High Street, so nice and quiet, really respectable, and no one knew my background at all. This was my first home, a nest I could make perfect for my family. I made it nice and homely, also making friends, going to someone else for coffee for the first time in my life. So I was in a nice place with all that but at the back of my mind – the front, really – all I could think of was Ben.

Dear Mandy

You're out! Can you believe it, you're out?

I'm so proud of you, I'm so proud looking back at how much strength you had to finally do it – actually managing to get away after going back that first time makes it even more incredible. He kept you trapped from the start, never thinking that you could get out of his web, always assuming you'd keep accepting it all, but the fire just grew and grew, didn't it? Once you had Pete, once you had that belief in what the future could hold, it was only a matter of time.

No one can ever imagine what it takes for a survivor to break free. Why didn't she leave? Why didn't she tell someone? Why didn't she just say no? These are the wrong questions and if you ask the wrong questions, you'll get the wrong answers.

Let's stop asking women why they didn't leave or why they didn't speak out.

Let's ask:

Why did he abuse that child?

Why did he keep raping her?

Why did he beat her senseless?

Why did he make her feel worthless, a slag, unlovable, useless?

Why did he choose to do all of these things? Why did HE do what HE did?

You have so much still to do, but you're on your way, Mandy – I'm watching and waiting, and I know you can do this.

12

'Incalculable Damage'

Calvin came back to us in the New Year and around about this time, I was referred to a women's counselling service, who then referred me on to another group, Leeds Incest Survivors Association (LISA). I hated that word 'incest' then just as much as I do now and it wasn't the right sort of thing for me at all. There was no counselling – it was all about punching pillows to get your anger out, which wasn't really going to help with what I or anyone else had been through. I only ever told people what I wanted them to know but writing this book is more than anything I've said in my life and certainly more than I ever told a so-called survivors' group. I always felt that no one knew what to do with me – there wasn't a group out there who could suddenly look at me and think, *ah, she's had kids with her father – we know exactly what to do!* I also thought there was no point talking about what had happened as it wouldn't change anything, would it? It was done, it was in the past. I never met any professional who seemed to be in the real world, they just simpered around me – they were all secure in their own little lives with no idea what to do about someone like me. Once I disclosed and felt they believed me, then I did trust Carol and Mark, my solicitor, more, but that didn't mean I would tell them everything.

By this point in 1990, it had been decided that Calvin and Ben should be placed in the same foster home as each other over Christmas, but the foster dad was a horrible man and vile to me when I visited. Mr Cunningham clearly didn't believe these 'sort of things' happened and that, as a grown woman, I should just face up to my responsibilities. He spoke down to me and any interaction we had was very short. He was a vicar, another Man of God who had very specific ideas about the place of women.

'They are your sons,' he would snap. 'As you can see, they're fine – we've looked after them well.' I was missing them so much one day so I called to ask how they were and he put the phone down on me. Mrs Cunningham was nice, she was lovely with them, but she was obviously under her husband's thumb. They did seem to have a very traditional relationship, which made me hope that she was the one caring for Ben and Calvin as I'm sure Mr Cunningham would have been cold with them. I did go to visit the boys whenever I was allowed but that's not right, is it?

You shouldn't need permission to see your own babies – however, that's the level I'd been dragged down to, that was my life, hoping that little bit of access wouldn't be taken away from me if I did something wrong. Not much makes me cry but when that man spoke to me it was as if my father was speaking to me again. He had no right. All he knew was the circumstances in which he was looking after my children, but he had decided I was the one in the wrong, I was the one who deserved his disgusting attitude. He looked down on me, barely acknowledging I even existed – he would walk out of the room if I walked into it. He made me feel like dirt. The Mandy I was then wouldn't say a word, but the Mandy I am now is furious that he did that. He treated my social worker Carol like a human being, but not me and I just accepted it; he treated me like everyone else did and I just took it all.

Calvin came back to me just after the New Year but I was still going back to the Cunninghams to see Ben. I remember taking him on a few trips, once to Blackpool, once to the zoo – always with Carol. They were never particularly nice days, not just because I felt I was being watched to see if I was a good enough mother, but because my little boy started crying when I left him at the end of the day and naturally I cried too.

He wants to be with me, I'd think every time it happened. I wasn't sure before, but I know now. *He wants to be with his mum and I want to be with him.* Before that, I hadn't been confident, given all the time he'd had away from me, but this was it, I would have to really fight to get Ben back. The doctors had always said he wouldn't walk, but he was managing a few steps by this time and I just knew if I could get him with me permanently, I would work so hard at making him even stronger and do all I could to keep him out of a wheelchair as he got older. I'd take him to every child development session, I'd do every exercise a hundred times a day, I'd work on every bit of apparatus – I'd prove that I was the best person to get my boy the best life possible.

Every time I went to the Cunninghams to see Ben, his face would light up as soon as I walked in the door. He'd take a few steps towards me then fall down, but I would encourage him all I could: 'Come on, Ben, you can do it! Come to your mum, there's a clever lad! Come on, come on!'

He grew in confidence and strength until one day he made it all the way over to my open arms. As my little boy collapsed into me, I could tell he was so proud and I had to hold back the tears, just telling him over and over again how well he had done, but wishing it had all been down to me. His tiny legs were twisted and his body was weak, but he'd done more than anyone had ever expected. Mrs Cunningham had genuinely done him proud but I wanted to be the one doing everything for him and I was holding on to the dream of the day when that would happen.

It was a strange feeling because all of the medical experts had told me that Ben didn't have the mental or physical capacity to do so many things, but I wasn't so sure. He'd been condemned to life in a wheelchair according to them, but now he was walking even though it was a struggle. He was recognising me and getting upset when I left, but I'd been coldly informed so many times that he didn't know I was his mother. It seemed as if it was something instinctive for him – he'd walk to me no matter how much of a struggle it was and it would break his heart when I left. He knew me, I just felt it in my bones, and I had to hold on to that to give me strength.

By the time the DNA results came through, I'd moved house to the nice maisonette in Yeadon, West Yorkshire, but was in no doubt about what they would be. How could I have any doubts? I'd been living with the reality since the moment Ben was born but Carol seemed to think it would be a shock to me.

'Do you want to sit down?' she asked. 'The results are in.' It sounded like some sort of reality show, as if it was all exciting rather than horrific. 'Well, you know that Ben is your dad's?'

Yes, Carol, I thought, *I do know that. I do know that my father planted his poison in me and Ben is suffering as a result of that.*

'Well, Calvin is your dad's too.'

I might have just said, 'Oh, right,' but inside I was

screaming, *no, neither of them are 'his', they're mine, they're nothing to do with him other than what he did to me to make them. They're my boys, my sons, my babies.*

'He'll be arrested and charged now, Mandy,' Carol informed me. 'There's no doubt about what he did. It'll go to court but who knows whether he'll plead guilty or not? I think he will because of the DNA evidence we have now, but I guess he could decide to go to trial. How do you feel?'

I shrugged. 'I knew it. It's no surprise to me – how *should* I feel?' There was never any answer to that question when I asked anyone. I had expected those results. I wasn't upset, I just boxed it all away as I always did – my way of dealing with everything.

'I don't know, Mandy, I just don't know,' Carol replied, coming over to me and wrapping me in her arms, visibly upset. 'You're like a daughter to me, you know that?'

After all I'd been through, I wasn't a 'huggy' person and she shouldn't have been getting so close to me, I don't think. She should have been keeping some sort of professional distance as my social worker, but, again, I just accepted everything. Carol used to visit me with her husband at weekends. She gave me her old furniture and I was really grateful for the practical help. She bought me food and had even said in the past that I should stay with her when Mum was kicking off. But I felt that was a bit much, a bit over-protective. I wasn't used to anyone looking out for me and I did wish she'd step back a little – it was too much, I felt suffocated. I was fine if she just saw me as another folder on her caseload, part of her job. However, I was starting to feel like more of a pet, almost an experiment which interested her. I don't think she understood, or wanted to understand, that I didn't need her to be anything other than my social worker. I wasn't crying out for her to be my mum in any way, I wanted to stand on my own two feet.

After she told me about the DNA test results, Carol stayed a few hours. I really just wanted to have the information and come to terms with it myself. She had others to deal with, but there didn't seem to be much recognition of that for her – she wanted to be at my house all the time, even at weekends.

Mum still kicked off, she still came and bothered me when she was drunk, so the police in Leeds soon got to know us. They were totally different to the ones I'd ever dealt with in Halifax. When they found out what was going on, they even had a collection and bought Calvin a pile of toys. It made me think that police could be nice and maybe something could be done now that the truth was known about the boys' paternity.

Even when Dad was arrested, I still wondered if he would wriggle his way out of it but I had this little glimmer of hope because these police officers were so nice to me. The CID bloke who had spoken to me knew Dad personally so I didn't trust the ones on that side at all. They were the ones who dealt with everything though as Dad was in Halifax.

All I could do was hope there were some good apples in the barrel there, not just the rotten ones I'd come across before.

The Halifax police told me that he had been arrested and I'd need to make a statement. We arranged a day and Carol drove me to Halifax Police Station.

'You'll have to tell them everything, Mandy,' she insisted as we made our way to the police station.

'I'm going to,' I replied.

'Everything though, every single thing,' she emphasised.

'I will, I'll leave nothing out,' I told her. I was a bit annoyed that she felt she had to say that, but I suppose she knew from my files that I'd withdrawn my allegations in the past and was keen that I didn't do so this time. All I knew was that I'd escaped from him, I'd never deny what he had done – it was time for me to make sure he paid the price.

Carol dropped me off outside the station and I was met by two policewomen, which was a relief – I didn't want to tell it all to a man. These women were really lovely, not in uniform, just dressed in what I would call 'normal' clothes. They took me to a very traditional interview room with two chairs on either side of a table and began to record it all.

'Tell us everything you can,' the older of the two said to me. 'Leave nothing out.'

We'd get to 32 pages by the time I was done eight hours later, but at that stage, I only had one thing to ask them – 'Is he here?'

The two policewomen exchanged a glance before one replied, 'He's in the cells, Mandy, but you've nothing to worry about. You'll be nowhere near him. He can't get to you.'

Before taking my statement, they told me that I could use any words I wanted to, words that I was more comfortable with, and they'd change them to the 'proper' ones later on. I still called my private parts my 'moo' and I've always called Dad's penis 'a Wilf' so I kept doing that and then they altered it. They were childish words, but I'd been a child, hadn't I?

The women were nice and made me feel at ease, letting me run with my story the way I wanted to, and I actually felt relief through the nerves. They just let me go on at my own pace, taking me to the police dining room for lunch before we went back to the interview room and finally got through everything.

As I was leaving, I looked down the corridor as I'd seen someone walking there out of the corner of my eye.

It was him.

I could only see the back of him, but I knew, I just knew. I recognised his hair. I recognised his shirt. And I certainly recognised the feeling in my stomach that I always had when he was near. Now, I think that was timed. I think someone he knew in the police had made sure that he was there when I came out and that I wasn't as safe as I'd been told I was.

'You said I wouldn't see him,' I whispered, terrified he would hear me and look in my direction.

'Honestly, Mandy, we had no idea this was going to happen – it *shouldn't* have happened.'

It was all about intimidation, I swear. I kept my eyes down so never had any idea whether he had looked my way at all. These days I look back on that Mandy who did that eight-hour interview and wonder how she managed it. I was a different person back then – I was timid, I was shy and for me to do all that was the start of the Mandy I am now. I was brave, I know that; I got my strength from knowing that it needed to be done and I couldn't ever go back. The only way to avoid that was if he was locked up, if he couldn't come looking for me and force me to come home. If he couldn't get me.

That Mandy of the past was gone. From that point on, I wasn't afraid to speak my mind. I'd stepped into a new power. I knew, for once, that someone believed me. My partner, Pete, had supported me through all of it, he was behind me, but he only knew some of it. Even reading this will tell him so many things that he's never known about.

It was now out of my control. I'd done my bit and it was up to other people to take it forward. Dad was arrested and charged in March 1991, the day after I gave my full statement. The papers I have state:

He admitted that he would plead guilty to one charge of indecent assault and two charges of incest. He had accepted that he was the father of both Ben and Calvin Meadows.

Mr Meadows was bailed [. . .] on condition

(a) Not to interfere with prosecution witnesses (Mandy):

or

(b) Not to see the two grandchildren.

They weren't his grandchildren though, were they? They were his sons. The fact that he had agreed to plead guilty and been arrested the day after my evidence was given suggests to me that when I saw the back of him walking down the police station corridor, it must have been then that he was giving his own statement. He was admitting to so very little: one charge of indecent assault and two charges of incest. As I've said before, I still hate that bloody word 'incest' – it suggests some form of relationship between abuser and abused, it hides the reality of a father raping his child, but that was what was written down. Did he really think that anyone would accept that he had only raped me twice and that on each of those occasions I'd got pregnant? I guess he did, I guess that's the horse he was backing.

On bail, he went back home to Mum, who welcomed him with open arms – in her eyes it was all my fault.

About a week after, I had a hospital check-up with Ben.

When I turned up, the receptionist said, 'Carol's been on the phone, Mandy. Can you ring her?'

I went out to the phone box and called my social worker.

She didn't mess about: 'He's taken an overdose, Mandy. We think he's going to come and find you. Stay in the office and we'll get in touch when we know what's happening.'

It was a terrifying thing to just drop on me and something I couldn't have predicted; all I needed to know was how to deal with it on a practical level.

'What are we going to do, Pete?' I asked.

'We'll just do as she says – we'll sit in the office and wait.'

It was the longest two hours I'd been through. I sat with Ben – and Calvin as he was with us too – gripping Pete's hand, petrified that Dad would burst through the door at any minute.

Finally, Carol called the office.

'What's happening?' I cried. 'Is he coming for me?'

She was calm as anything. 'No, it's fine. Crisis over, you're safe.'

'What? How do you know? Why did you think he was coming for me and now everything's fine?'

She sighed. 'It just is, Mandy – there's nothing to worry about.'

Well, I wouldn't have been worried if she hadn't got me all riled up. Maybe he would have come to Leeds, maybe he would have tried to kill me before he killed himself. This man, my father, who had raped me for years, who had now taken an overdose, was the one who was getting the support from Social Services while I was basically left to my own devices. No one was checking up on me other than Carol. I know that he was also getting support from The Salvation Army – he'd told them he accepted full responsibility and they were standing by him, as was Mum.

My father was bailed again at the start of May 1991, about six weeks after he had been charged, but, again, no one told me. One of the conditions was that he would stay with his parents, who still adored him, and I'm sure they blamed me too.

In July 1991, I was given full care of Ben – until that point, we'd all been doing a transition where he was with me most of the time but he went back to the foster parents every so often. I was observed to make sure that I could care for my own son and they finally agreed that he could be with me 24/7. It was around this time that I also went to Victim Support in Leeds in the hope that they could give me some support.

In the files, it states:

Shortly before Mr Meadows appeared in Court, there was an indication, via the Probation Service, that he was going to deny any sexual activity with his daughter until she became 18, in the hope of reducing the sentence.

I suppose he could try for that, given the boys were born after I'd turned 18, but that isn't the part of the files that kicked me so hard. It was this extract:

[. . .] *there was information from a Hospital Psychiatrist's notes referring to Mrs Jennifer Meadows, in which she referred to her husband's sexual activity with Mandy when she was only 11 years of age.*

I've reread that so many times.

[. . .] *she referred to her husband's sexual activity with Mandy when she was only 11 years of age.*

She *knew*.

Mum knew all along.

When she'd walked into my bedroom and found Dad raping me, when he had said 'sorry' to her and she'd said he had nothing to be sorry about, that wasn't the start of her knowing, or the start of her dismissing his actions: she'd known since I was 11. Seeing those notes made me realise that all my feelings, all my suspicions, were correct: she knew and she didn't care.

That was my mother; that was the woman who should have cherished me, loved me and kept me safe.

I've thought of this as a mother (how can a woman ever

know her husband is doing that to her daughter?) and it beggars belief that she could have turned a blind eye but as a *human being*, how can anyone justify it? She knew he was raping me, she put me on the Pill, she was delighted when my father made me pregnant. It's the most disgusting thing a mother can do. As far as I'm concerned, she should have been charged as well. As far as I'm concerned, she gave birth to me so that he could rape me – that's how I feel.

The least she could have done was to kick him out, but she wasn't ever bothered to do that. She had this strange combination of adoration for him but also not wanting him anywhere near her. It's like Myra Hindley, it's like Rose West. She was wrapped up in him, she was under his spell, but I don't think she wanted anything physical at all. Over and above everything, she cared more for him than me. She wasn't controlled by him, she colluded in my abuse.

Dad was charged in March 1991. My solicitor, Mark, had taken a statement from Mum when Dad's court case began the following year and found out he had done some awful stuff to her.

Dad denied anything happened until I was 18, yet my mother told a hospital psychiatrist she knew of the abuse since I was 11. Surely patient confidentiality overrides that? There can't be any secrecy where a child's safety is concerned – but there was. The psychiatrist knew, it was passed to another psychiatrist, who completed a Court Report, they all had the information ... Mum was, in effect, a witness, yet there was so little done to address the enormity of it all.

Dad appeared at the Crown Court in September 1991, six months after his arrest, having had six months out enjoying his freedom. Thankfully, he pleaded guilty – to very little – but at least I didn't have to give evidence.

I was still in contact with my friend whose parents owned the chip shop I'd worked in, who was the first person I'd ever told. She rang me when she saw my story in the newspaper.

'That's it, Mandy – he's been sent to prison.'

I felt as if I could finally breathe but no one official, not even my social worker Carol got in touch to tell me that he had been found guilty. Instead, my friend sent me the newspaper clipping and I held on to it for dear life.

In the only legal and medical files I've been able to find, it says:

Mr Keith Meadows appeared at Leeds Crown Court on 10.9.1991 and was given a three-year prison sentence by Judge Saville. Mr Meadows admitted four charges of incest with his daughter between October 1982 and January 1990. He denied two charges of incest which Judge David Saville ordered to remain on file. He was quoted as saying, 'Incest by a father with a daughter is always a serious matter because it inevitably involves a father taking advantage of the

experience and innocence of the daughter. You used
her for your own sexual desires and the result is that
she may have suffered emotional and psychological
damage quite incalculable.'

Admitting four charges over a period of seven and a half
years was laughable – four times in almost eight years? And
two children from that? Did they honestly believe that my
dad had just done it four times, that he had kept away from
me all of the other times?

When I read the newspaper clipping that my friend sent
me, all I felt was guilt. Guilt that I'd sent my own father to
prison. But I did think, *at least he can't hurt me anymore –*
I can move forward, he can't get me, he can't hurt me. I did
think Mum would come and get me though, but I'd moved
by that time and hoped that would be enough.

He got three years – which meant he'd be out in 18
months.

In those 18 months, I needed to get on with my life. The
first thing to do was change the surname of Ben and Calvin
to that of Pete's. I'd long stopped using mine to distance
myself from my father. I was terrified that he might put in
a claim for the boys and try for access, but he never did –
it doesn't stop rapists, I've since learned they do it all the
time, but thankfully, he didn't go down that route.

I also got Ben back. The smallest thing and the biggest
thing. As I've said, I'd been able to visit when he was at the

Cunninghams and I had built a relationship with him, but actually having him returned to me full-time, permanently, seemed like a lottery win.

I'll never forget the date – 4 July 1992.

We'd been in the new house for about a year and that had been one of the conditions imposed as necessary before my son could come home, but it took longer because of waiting to see what was happening with Dad and the lack of certainty around that. On the morning I woke up knowing that my little boy was coming back to me, it felt like Christmas – well, I say I woke up, but I don't think I slept at all. My house is always cleaned to within an inch of its life anyway, but I went round it all again just to make sure – you could have operated on every surface, they were that pristine! Everything had to be perfect.

The doorbell went at around 10 a.m. and I took a deep breath: this was it. This was the moment I'd been told wouldn't happen, when my child was given to other people, when he was allowed to stay with my parents, when I had the words of my parents in my head – *useless, you don't know how to be a mother, you're poison, everything you touch is ruined*. Not any longer. In just a few seconds, I'd have Pete, Ben and Calvin all here with me and our life would stretch out golden in front of us.

Carol was there, holding Ben's hand when I opened the door. I whisked him up in my arms and he started laughing, saying, 'Mum! Mum!' over and over again. I have to hand it to the foster carer – any time Ben called her 'Mum', she corrected him and now he had no doubt who I was.

'You're home, Ben, you're home!' I laughed along with him. He was able to toddle about by then and I just followed him around, showing him where he would sleep every night, right next to his baby brother. I think Calvin found it a little hard at first as he was used to having us to himself for so long, but they both settled so quickly and became good friends.

I was the happiest mum: I had learned to love Ben and he loved me back. I had my boys, I had my family – something I had never thought could happen. When they went to bed that night, I don't think I sat down for more than five minutes. I kept popping in and out of their room, watching them sleep, stroking their cheeks, kissing the tops of their heads. I knew how to love now and I would never let that go.

I was so happy with them all but it would be wrong to say that I never thought of Dad. There were moments when I even felt guilty that I was the one responsible for putting him in jail, then I'd give myself a shake and think, *come on, Mandy, he did it – he put himself in jail with what he did*. I think that happens to a lot of survivors – we can't help but feel it was our fault if there is some sort of justice because we've been told for so long that if we disclose, the family will be ripped apart and when, *if*, it does happen, those words don't disappear, they still have power.

In prison, I know that he worked as head of the cleaning department, again giving himself authority, again being the big 'I Am'. In fact, in one of the notes from the Social Services records, it says:

Mandy feels that he has again got people and professionals on his side. She feels the family still blame her and he does nothing convincing to change this.

I had a new social worked by now called Anji, who was lovely. She came to see me one day and I could just tell something had happened by the look on her face.

'Mandy, this might shock you but your dad's probation officer has been in touch. As part of his rehabilitation, he wants you to visit him in prison so he can apologise.'

My response was instant, I didn't have to even think: 'No! No, I'm not doing that.'

'I completely understand,' she said, 'but you don't have to decide at the moment – think about it.'

'I don't have to – I'm not giving him the satisfaction, I'll never do that.'

'Are you sure?'

I nodded.

'Well, do you mind if I go?'

'I don't see why you'd want to, but fill your boots, visit him if you like,' I told her.

When Anji came back to see me the week after, I knew she'd seen him for what he was.

'What an awful man!' she said, half-whispering. 'He scared me so much, Mandy. He was lording it over me, telling me all I needed to know about him and how wonderful he was. You were right, you were 100 per cent right. I'm so glad you didn't go.'

'I know him, I know what he's like,' I said.

'He just wanted you to go there and see him, I know that now – there was never going to be any pretence at an apology.'

'Control – that's all he wants,' I scoffed. 'I'm just glad someone else has seen it now.'

Again, the notes make it clear that I had always known what he was up to:

> *Mandy says Keith needs to control – he needs to control and fails to take in anybody's needs but his own. Until there is a demonstration that this has changed, she feels there is no way forward and does not want any contact. To push this at present would be to minimise Keith Meadows' offence against her.*

Over those 18 months when my father was in jail, I concentrated on my family, but I also started to tell people what had happened. A lot of people didn't want to know, they still don't. I remember saying to one woman at a mum and toddler group, 'This is what happened to me.' I didn't go into detail, but when I'd finished, she picked up her coffee cup and moved to another table. She never said a single word to me again at any of the other group meetings I went to from that day forwards. Again, that made me think it was my fault, that I had to carry the shame. It must be me, I must have led him on. I must have been part of it willingly and she was disgusted by me. After that, I stopped telling people.

I was guilty too. I must have done something to make him do that.

I also felt so ashamed that I stayed. Why did I go back after I first escaped? If someone was telling me my story, I'd ask why. I'd ask why they hadn't kept running. I was so scared of him, of people not believing me and of having the kids taken away from me that it was too much the first time, just too much to cope with – so back I went, back to the hell of it all.

Social Services watched me all the time. I guess there's always that belief in some people that the abused go on to abuse. Ben was obviously still getting a lot of medical care and his problems were changing. One of the things he would do is withhold his poo so that when he did go, he had to strain terribly, often crying in pain. One day, the usual doctor for Ben was busy so we met with a locum, who examined him as we watched.

I tried to tell her what was wrong with him, to summarise

what was in the files as I knew a new doctor might not have had the chance to read them all, but she continued to look at every single part of my son, including his bottom. Covering him up again, she looked at me and stated, 'This boy has been abused.'

'What?' I exclaimed. 'He's never out of my sight! He hasn't been abused, he couldn't have been.'

'I'm telling you, that child has been abused. I can see it when I look at his bottom.'

'And I can tell you with every fibre of my being that he has NOT been abused! I want to see Ben's usual doctor, I want to see him now!' I insisted.

Dr Ferguson was called. As I sat soothing Ben, waiting for the doctor who I could only pray would tell this new medic what was going on, it felt like a lifetime. I was always terrified that the kids were going to be taken from me and this was just another potential threat. But Dr Ferguson explained everything and made it clear that there was no abuse going on, that Ben had been straining for months and that as an expert, she knew for sure my little boy was in no danger from me. I still felt so small though and that I was at the mercy of anyone who could come along and just take my babies from me.

I was still blaming myself about what had happened and there was no support, not even much sympathy, for what I had gone through. I remember my GP even saying to me, 'Well, prison isn't a very nice place for a man to be, is it?

He won't be enjoying that.' I hoped not, but what an awful thing for a professional to say to a victim.

My whole family had pulled away from me – I was the one who was in the wrong, I was the one who had brought all of this about. Mum was standing by him, the love of her life, and I was the one out in the cold. I didn't care, I was busy making my own family.

13

The Mother I Was
Made to Be

Pete and I wanted our own family and decided to try for a baby in the middle of all this. It sounds awful, but Ben and Calvin were never Pete's kids, and I know the way they came into the world meant he could never feel that way about them – I had certainly had my difficulties too. It was time for us to take the next step and have a child made from love but I had my concerns.

'What if I can't love it, Pete? What if I can't love any baby the way a mother should? I don't want to bring another child into the world if it won't be loved.'

'But you would love it,' he told me. 'I know you would.'

'I don't see how you can be so certain – I can't, so how can you?'

'I know you, Mandy. I know you don't think you're enough for Ben and Calvin, but I see you with them,

I see you do everything a mother should, and even if you question yourself, I know that you would do anything for them.'

'I'll never get over the fact that they're here because of what he did to me though ...' I admitted.

Pete held me in his arms and said, 'You don't have to, you just have to keep on being the best mum you can be for them – and open yourself up to us having a baby together that will come from how we feel about each other. It'll be different, it'll be your baby, nothing to do with what happened before and you can be the mum you want to be, no one else will be telling you what to do. Take your time, it'll happen if it's meant to happen.'

And it did. I got pregnant a few months before Dad was sentenced and I was still feeling that I might not be able to love this baby at first, but once it started moving, everything changed. This baby was mine and when I felt the little kicks and flutters, it felt like we were in our own little world together. It was the first time I had really thought about how incredible it all was.

Charlotte was born in March 1992 and I adored her from the moment I set eyes on her. When she was handed to me, all I could do was marvel at her fingers and toes, her blonde hair, every part of her so perfect, but there was also a part of me saying, *you're being like a proper mum now, Mandy!* All I could think was, *I love you, you're amazing.* The other difference was Pete. I'd never seen a real dad look at one of my children like that before. It was just pure love in his eyes that day, for Charlotte and for me.

I stayed in hospital overnight and didn't sleep a wink, I just stared at my daughter. Every time she made the slightest whimper, I picked her up; I'd never done that with Ben and Calvin. It sounds awful, but I felt that I was being a mum for the first time: she was pure. I'd never expected that rush of love and I was overwhelmed by what I felt for my little girl. I'd thought I'd be stuck in that house with Dad forever, having one disabled baby after another, filled with his poison and never escaping, but here I was, a proper mum with a beautiful baby made out of what Pete and I shared together.

Charlotte was such a contented baby and I never let her out of my arms if it could be avoided. She always had to be with me even though I knew there was no one around who would hurt her in this new life I had. But I still had this overriding feeling that I had to keep her safe, I had to protect her from anything and everything. I think I was scared because she was a girl. What would happen when Dad got out of prison, what would happen if he decided to come and get her? I tried to just focus on the lovely relationship Charlotte's own father was building with her but my past was there, niggling at me, telling me things. I never let Pete bathe her. I trusted him, I knew he wouldn't abuse but *what if, what if* ran through my mind the whole time.

The news seemed to be full of abuse stories. Every day, there was another one about terrible things being done to children and I wondered whether it would ever change. There were always reports of current court cases with young children, but also more and more relating to historical cases – one of the things I despised the most was the idea that Dad must have thought he had got away with it all, just as all of those other men must have thought so too. It was wrong. Not just what he'd done, but that he had never faced any consequences for so long.

One night, I felt as if something had changed when I was lying in bed thinking about it all. I'd spent so long being scared, so long feeling a weight on my shoulders, but, as if a switch had been flicked, I knew it was time for me to finally reclaim myself, to acknowledge what I had been through and become the Mandy I needed to be for my own children.

The light from a big fat moon was streaming in the bedroom window and I could still hear birds singing outside, even though it was night. Summer had started early and it felt as though everything was full of hope. It was just before midnight and Pete was fast asleep. I closed my eyes, took a deep breath and rubbed his shoulder.

'Are you awake?' I whispered.

'I am now,' he groaned. 'Sort of …'

'I need to fight, Pete,' I told him. 'I need to – and now's the time.'

He sat up, startled. 'What do you mean, you're going to fight? Your dad's been done for this.'

'It's not about that, it's about something bigger,' I told him. 'It's not about moving past what he did – I don't want anyone to think I can just put that behind me, but I can decide where I go from here. I can decide that, even though he still frightens me, I can be a good mum. I don't have to always think of the poison he put in me. Ben is just Ben, Calvin is just Calvin. I can't change any of that, but I can be the best version of me possible for them and for Charlotte, and for any other little ones we might have in the future.'

I didn't feel upset or tearful as I got up and went into the living room. This felt right. I knew I was choosing to march into battle and that it would be a long, possibly painful journey, but it still seemed like the right choice. It had been building for so long – years possibly – but it was Charlotte who had finally shown me that now was the time to take this step. The love I had for her was so strong, I wanted to draw on it and make the best life possible. So often, as I looked at her in my arms, or curling safely into her dad, there were times when I couldn't help but think of the life I needed to give her: she would be safe and she would be loved.

She would have everything I'd never had.

My existence had been one of fear and terror, never knowing what would be done to me, never knowing when the cruelty and abuse would begin. Always, always knowing that the only thing I could guarantee was that it *would* happen again. That nobody cared enough to stop it and that 'he' would just keep using me for his own needs until something happened. What he had done to me had coloured my whole life. I hated him for that and while that hatred would never go away, there was a stronger emotion which I needed to harness – my love for my children and Pete could get me through anything. I could find the strength for this.

Pete appeared beside me just as I thought of him, as if he knew.

'I hate what he did to you,' he announced. 'I hate that he hurt you in so many ways. I hate that what he did still hurts you. I hate that he got away with it for so long – and I am absolutely, 100 per cent, with you forever. I love you, Mandy, I'll always be here for you.'

I smiled. 'I do seem to be stuck with you!'

'We're stuck with each other – and that's how it should be,' he said, kissing me on the forehead.

Eleven months later, we did it all again when Rebecca was born! I had all this love to give and now that I'd seen what it was like with Charlotte, I just wanted it over and over again. Which is exactly what happened – after Charlotte came Rebecca in February 1993, then Nathan came along in May 1995, followed by Joe in 1996 before having a rest for a while! Millie appeared in 2001 – she was an accident, to be honest, as I'd said I wouldn't have any more after being hospitalised for 11 weeks with placenta praevia while pregnant with Joe, but then I got addicted to babies again! Phoebe was born in August 2002, again just 11 months after her sister, then Conan in September 2005, Angel in 2006 and Blue in 2007. I needed a family, I needed to give love and to be a proper mum. I wanted my children to never be hurt, I wanted to protect them, and I never let them play out. I gave them enough siblings so that they always had someone to play with, I never allowed them sleepovers – but it wasn't enough.

There was more shocking news to come a few years later, when I was 42. We discovered that Pete's younger brother, Richard, was a paedophile too and Pete was the one to put it all together. He'd been visiting family and noticed that one of the young lads wouldn't leave Richard's side. When he came home, he said to me, 'It was like watching you with your dad when I used to see you in town together – that lad was stuck like glue. There's something not right, it's like that boy is proper scared of him – what should I do?'

'You tell someone,' I said immediately. 'You get this sorted.'

Pete told Social Services and when we went home afterwards, our daughter Rebecca overheard us talking about it.

'Grace told me he'd been at her a few years ago,' she said.

'Why the hell didn't you say something?' I shouted back at her.

'She asked me not to, she asked me to keep it to myself.'

All those secrets again, all those lies.

It didn't take long to unravel and, again, we found out that Pete's mum had known all along. My mother-in-law, the grandmother of my children, was just the same as my own mum. Ignoring it all but knowing full well what was going on. Richard had been abusing for 20 years and I hadn't picked up on it at all. He was the youngest of seven and he would babysit for Pete's whole family, getting the kids to play games that soon turned into something much more sinister.

But I was to blame too: I didn't notice what was going on right in front of me. One weekend, Richard was looking after his sister's house and Calvin was visiting, along with the rest of us.

'Can Calvin stay a bit longer?' Richard had asked. 'Just to play video games?'

And to my shame, I'd said yes. He was Pete's brother, he was Calvin's uncle. I should have known that it doesn't matter if it's family – a paedophile doesn't care, they have no boundaries as I knew only too well, and I will *never* forgive myself for allowing it to happen. I thought I'd been so careful, I thought I was protecting them all, but abuse always seems to find a way. It wasn't just once – not that I'm saying that would have been all right – but it emphasises that he knew what he was doing, this wasn't a one-off. This man came into my family, inserted himself into our lives, and he had done that. They all knew what had happened to me and yet they still allowed it. I wanted to kill him.

Richard was arrested and was eventually found guilty and sentenced to 15 years in prison for all the family members he'd abused. He pleaded not guilty and both Calvin and Pete had to testify. I needed to move past it and concentrate on what we had, not what could have been, had Richard not been caught.

Once I had my 'gang', all my babies, I did start to feel I was a good mum – and Ben was doing quite well too. Mainstream school didn't really work and he had to go to a special school, but his mobility wasn't too bad and I didn't need to give 24/7 care. Ben needed an eye kept on him and some help, but he could feed himself and get around a bit. Now, however, his fine motor skills have almost disappeared and he needs me constantly. When the kids were small, I did have time to focus on the other children as well, not just my eldest. It was amazing to have such a big family, it was hectic and there was always something happening. I didn't get a moment to myself and that was just how I liked it: if I was constantly busy, I didn't have time to think about what had happened to me and my children.

Of course, as the older ones started to question things, they'd ask, 'Why is Ben the way he is?' How do you tell your children the answer to that question? I guess the big kids just passed the information down to the little ones and all I can ever remember was them not understanding why anyone would be horrible to me. They always knew Ben was different, but as time went on, they knew why. It was harder with Calvin though because he was being told he had been born from rape.

He was about 12 when I had to have that conversation. We lived in Leeds and were thinking of going back to Halifax. I said to Pete, 'Calvin has to know – if we go back there, so many people have that information and I don't want it coming from someone else.'

Any time Calvin rowed with Pete, he would say, 'You're not my dad anyway,' and I felt he just knew in his heart. Pete had been around since he was little and although he'd always loved, cared and provided for him, their relationship became strained as Calvin grew older.

The only words I could come up with were, 'Something bad happened to me when I was younger, Calvin, and you need to know about it. My dad abused me and he's your dad.'

'Is that why Ben's like he is?'

'Yeah – yeah, it is.'

He didn't ask a single thing until he was older. We'd come to Halifax one day for some clothes, with the two younger boys, and we saw my parents. Mum stared and stared at me as she always did, as they both did. I was petrified. Pete hustled me into a shop with the three boys who were with us and Nathan asked, 'Who are they?'

'That's my mum and dad,' I had to say.

When we got back, Nathan told Calvin, who asked him, 'What does she look like?'

'A nonce,' his little brother told him.

Calvin blames me. At one point, a few years ago, he put something up on his Facebook and it acknowledged who his father was. That was the first time he had ever done that – *I've finally seen the face of the scum of the earth*, he wrote. *The one who raped his own daughter.*

When we moved from Blackpool to Halifax in 2013, Calvin came to visit twice. He was 22 years old by now and had moved out and he'd go for walks on his own, which I found strange as he didn't know his way around the place. I have no idea where he went or who he saw – and I'd only be making wild guesses. When he came back, he'd sit there in silence, then leave. I know he finds it difficult – he messages his sisters and tells them what he thinks of me. He once said that he'd spoken to my mum and she'd said that everything was my fault, but that was after I found out that Mum had died, so he definitely hadn't spoken to her. Maybe he was just finding an excuse to say what he thought? At one point I found out that he'd taken my dad's name and I was in pieces about that. He looks so much like him – they're like twins – and I'll be honest, I can't stand it. That's a terrible thing for me to say but as he gets older, he's getting to the age Dad was when he started abusing me. It's not his fault, but it's awful. How many women are there out there who feel like that? How many of them look at the faces of their children and see their rapist? It scares me, takes me back to a place I never want to go.

But I've come to terms with it now. As long as my kids keep in touch with Calvin and let me know he's OK, I can deal with it. I love him, I really do, but it's hard, really hard. My dad is still alive and I wouldn't know if Calvin has had any contact with him but I really hope not – I know how manipulative my father can be.

I need to go back here for a bit – I feel like there are two strands to my story around this time of my life because I was developing into the best mum I could possibly be, with Pete by my side and all our little ones coming along quickly, but there was also the continuing issue of my dad.

He'd got out in early 1993 – I was at home in Yeadon with the three kids, Ben, Calvin and Charlotte, when the phone rang.

'I know where you are. I *will* come and get you.'

I put the phone down straight away – of course, I knew it was him. After closing all the curtains, I sat in the room with the kids until Pete came back. I went to the solicitor's the next day and they told me they'd get an injunction out against him. The day it was heard, I had to go and wait to be taken into the judge's room.

'I had this awful dream last night,' I admitted to Catherine from the solicitor's as we stood there. 'I was here, in this room, and so was Dad – and he stabbed me.'

'Well, that's not going to happen, Mandy. Don't worry,' she told me.

But then he was there: he was there in a flash.

Out of nowhere, my father appeared with his solicitor in the corridor where we were waiting and Catherine had to jump in front of me. I honestly thought my dream was going to come true, it had been a premonition. Although I kept my eyes on the floor, I could practically feel the heat of his eyes boring into me. We were called into the judge's room and told to sit down – Dad was no more than a few seats away from me. I didn't look at him once. How in the world could that have been allowed? How could it have been seen as right that he could be sat there beside me when he had just got out of jail for raping me and was now threatening to come and get me?

The injunction was granted and he was told that if he didn't stay away, he'd be sent back to prison for the rest of his sentence. He never rang me again but when the injunction ran out a year later, I saw him following me in the street once or twice.

I went back to work in the chip shop and he would follow me in his car as I walked there. He'd follow me in a blue Salvation Army van (they'd welcomed him back with open arms, which shouldn't have surprised me, but it did). If I went out for a break at lunchtime, he'd follow me as I went home. He'd follow me to the supermarket, he'd appear in car parks, outside shops, everywhere. Just staring, just staring at me. He never said a word but it was incredibly intimidating and I still thought he would stab me, given the chance. I'd sense him wherever I went and I was always right: if I thought he was there, he would be there. I also still thought he would take Ben and Calvin. In fact, I still think to this day he would take Ben from me if he could. He still follows me, I still see him. Every time he appears, I just have to come home. I don't know if he follows me home – I keep my head down, I'd never voluntarily look at him but I also never want to have to run away ever again. I'll stand my ground but he remains obsessed with me.

But the Mandy I wanted to be tried to move on. My heart felt it was coming out of my chest any time my father was nearby. However, I was determined not to lose any more of my life to him. Anyway, there was Ben to look after and he was getting worse. I was sick of saying there was something wrong with him – everyone would always say, 'It's just Ben, it's how he is.' When he was 15, in 2008, I googled all his symptoms again and decided to push for some sort of diagnosis. I then went to my GP, told him what had happened with Dad and he fast-tracked us an appointment to a consultant clinician in Manchester.

The clinician's letter said:

Dear Mandy and Peter

I promised I would write you a letter following your visit with Ben to the genetic clinic as you very much wanted to know whether a specific diagnosis could be made to explain Ben's problems. As I understood it from Mandy, she felt that establishing a diagnosis for Ben would be helpful to know what to expect from him in the future and also to be able to have an answer when filling in forms or when responding to people's questions about, 'What is wrong with Ben?' Ben and his brother were born as the result of prolonged abuse by Mandy's own father and it has always been suspected that Ben's difficulties are due to this. We know that about half of the children born as a result of such abuse have problems but half do not.

Ben was noted to have a hole in his heart and to be a floppy baby. He had several chest infections when he was small and was transferred to a paediatrician in Halifax. You remember that when he was one year of age he was still floppy and could not hold his head up. You also remember that his feet tended to turn in and you tried to massage these. He was slow walking and crawling and did not in fact walk until he was two and a half years of age. Ben has always been a tall boy but has had problems often in maintaining his weight. He has had hearing problems and needed grommets, and also has a squint and was short-sighted. Ben can write at about the level of a five-year-old. He does struggle with money and would not be able to go to the shop on his own.

I examined Ben. His head does look large and he has a certain look to him, with his forehead tending to slant downwards with a longish face. When he stands up, his chest looks narrow and he has a rather stooped posture. His fingers are long and he cannot fully straighten his fingers from his knuckle joints. He is worse on his right-hand side. His feet are better than they used to be but they are rather flat and he has a tendency to curl his toes. In discussion with you, I told you that the combination of learning, difficulties, heart problems in the past, squint, hands and feet problems, and his distinctive face are all likely to be linked to an underlying genetic cause or syndrome.

Because of the circumstances of Ben's conception, we can be virtually certain that he has a rare recessive syndrome. The risk of a recessive disorder goes up steeply the closer the relationship between a child's parents. I suggested we use the term 'recessive syndrome with learning and joint problems' for Ben. If more information was needed, you could then go on to say that he had a double dose of a faulty gene.

We had a definition now: *'recessive syndrome with learning and joint problems'*.

I always remember that consultant saying, 'You're not alone – I've seen this before, I've seen quite a few girls in your situation.' That amazed me: how many fathers were doing this to their daughters?

From that point on, whenever I attended any hospital or medical appointment with Ben, I would tell them, 'Ben has recessive syndrome with learning and joint problems,' or say, 'I'll write it down for you.' To this day, I mostly do the latter, passing over a note which says *'I was raped by my father and Ben is the product of that'*. They rarely acknowledge it, they just move on. With a lot of new appointments, they've rarely heard of his syndrome either. They look at me as if I'm making it up and I wish I was, I really wish I was, but this is my son's life, this is my past, and while no one would choose it, we all have to play the hand we're given and I promised every day afresh that I would fight for Ben with every breath in my body. I was his mum now 100 per cent, there was no doubt about that.

14

Charlotte

Life was frantic with all the kids – and I loved every minute of it. It was madness and it was brilliant. We'd moved to Blackpool in 2003 just to get away from everything that had bad associations for us and to try and avoid bumping into my family. The whole place is filled with tourists pretty much all the time so we never really went out, it was too full of visitors. We'd go to St Ann's instead as it's a much nicer resort and we'd have lovely days there. But there was another reason: Mum. Once social media took off, she had a way of tracking me down and I'd get friend requests and messages from her all the time. I blocked her as soon as they came in, but she tried to find us in other ways – I soon found out that she was following all the hotels and B&Bs in Blackpool. I could see that she was 'liking' them all and presumably looking for check-ins or maybe posts to say one of us was working there. It was really odd behaviour and I just felt I never wanted my kids out of my sight in case she found them. Once they were older and knew, they could take more care, but while they were entirely dependent on me and Pete, I had to be incredibly careful.

They'd all play in the garden with their trampoline and slide – in a big family like ours there's always someone to muck about with. I was in my element. Being a mum was everything to me, it still is. Life had to be like a military operation with cooking, cleaning, school; it still is as half of them are still living at home! Every time I had a baby, I'd get up in the middle of the night to clean as I wanted everything spotless and it was easier without anyone else getting under my feet. Pete did all the cooking as I'm rubbish and we made a great team together. I loved them all so much but there was also an element of keeping my life so busy that I wouldn't have time to think.

I did still think of Charlotte as the baby who had opened my heart to knowing what it was to be a proper mum and she was turning into the most wonderful young woman, 19 years old by now. She wasn't just funny, loving and beautiful, she was smart too and began studying criminology to be a solicitor, the first in either of our families to go to university. She was perfect – but she was a drama queen! There were only 11 months between her and Rebecca and I think that's what started Charlotte wanting attention, she didn't get enough time for her! She was a gobby cow but everyone loved her.

She had a boyfriend called Mickey, who she'd been with for about a year and she was more at his house than ours. He lived with his dad and siblings, and Charlotte stayed there a lot. When she fell out with Mickey, she went to stay with an older friend of his family because she was close to that woman's little daughter. In fact, she looked after her so much that I used to comment on it. I do think that this woman, Joanie, took advantage of Charlotte's good nature. She was just too kind-hearted – she'd even let a friend take out a phone in her name when they couldn't get credit and they'd ripped her off by never paying the monthly contract. She'd do anything for anyone.

Charlotte loved Mickey, she really did, but they had a massive row one night and she went to a cheap hotel just to get her own headspace. She rang me from there and I asked her, 'When are you coming home?'

'I think I'll come back in the morning, actually,' she told me. 'Get you to look after me for a while.'

'Do you need looking after?' I asked.

'I think I do – to be honest, Mum, I've taken some paracetamol. They didn't seem to agree with me, but I'll be OK. I'll see you in the morning,' she told me.

'OK, love you,' I replied.

'Love you, Mum,' she answered.

I'd never hear her voice again.

She didn't come home in the morning but I just assumed she'd gone back to Mickey's or Joanie's. The next day was Angel's birthday and Charlotte still hadn't been in touch so Rebecca said, 'I'm going to ring that woman,' by which she meant Joanie.

'Yeah, she's here,' Rebecca was told, 'but she doesn't look very well. I think she's eaten some chicken nuggets that have made her poorly – she can't really come to the phone just now.' Rebecca didn't get to speak to her, but we just thought, if she has food poisoning, the last thing she'll feel like doing is having a chat.

On the Thursday, we'd just finished watching a film and were making bacon butties when there was a knock at the door: it was the police.

'What's she done now?' I asked, laughing. A couple of weeks before, Charlotte had been absolutely pissed and the police had told her to watch herself, so I just assumed she'd been up to some nonsense again. It's funny that I thought it was to do with Charlotte though when they turned up – my mind went to her automatically.

'Can we come in?' asked the younger policewoman. When they did, she announced, 'Charlotte's in hospital.'

My stomach lurched immediately. 'Why?'

'I'm so sorry, Mandy, but she's in a critical condition. Get dressed, you have to come to hospital.'

'I'm not going,' said Pete. 'I can't.'

I went upstairs to quickly get ready; I don't know what

the policewoman said to him, but Pete had his coat on by the time I got back.

Rebecca appeared from her room, wondering what was going on, and I had to tell her that Charlotte was in hospital and her face just fell. The police took us to the hospital where our little girl was in Intensive Care. Charlotte was completely yellow, unresponsive, with tubes coming out of her everywhere I looked. My child, my first girl, looked unrecognisable from the young woman I knew and adored. I didn't cry, I just held her hand and kissed her face – and prayed to a God I didn't believe in that this wasn't as hopeless as it looked.

A doctor by the side of the bed said, 'We've been told that your daughter took 20 paracetamol?'

'She told me she'd taken some and they hadn't agreed with her – was it really 20?'

He nodded.

'She was sick though. She vomited them all up and it was days ago,' I added.

'Unfortunately, Charlotte had a terrible reaction to the drugs,' he informed me coldly. 'They were too much for her system. Can you come with me for a moment, please?' He took us to another room. 'We do have a liver available in Leeds, but we feel that Charlotte is too far gone for a transplant to be successful.'

'What do you mean, "too far gone"?' I said. 'You need to do it! You need to get her a transplant!'

'She wouldn't make it, I'm afraid.'

'Don't talk rubbish! Get her ready. Please. Please get her ready,' I begged.

'I'm so sorry,' he said, quietly. 'There's nothing we can do for Charlotte, it's too late.'

She was moved to another room quite soon after that and we were advised that the older kids should come to see her and say goodbye. I went home and told them all – Pete couldn't do it.

'Charlotte's not coming home,' I told the little ones, holding them close. 'She's not coming back to us, she's gone to live with the angels.' Each of them did what they had to do to get through those moments and it wouldn't be right for me to put their grief on the page, but I do remember them all just begging me to make her better – because that's what I do, I make things better. But I couldn't this time, I couldn't do it for Charlotte and I couldn't do it for our family.

When I went back, another doctor told me that if they'd seen Charlotte earlier, they could have saved her. If I'd gone to get her the night she called me, maybe things would have been different. I was in bits and also, I couldn't help but think if Joanie hadn't decided she had eaten dodgy chicken nuggets, Charlotte might have been saved. At that point, Charlotte was basically dying in front of her, all her organs were failing and she only had hours before she'd be in a coma. I just wanted to wind the clock back and change things – I was clinging to anything, anyone to blame.

Word got out so quickly and before I knew it, lots of Charlotte's friends were coming in to say their goodbyes and then Pete and I were with her that final night, knowing, just knowing what the next day would bring. How can I explain that, how can I describe what it's like to spend those precious moments with your child at the end of their life? I looked at my poor girl and remembered what she had given to me – she'd shown me how to be a mother, a real mother who loved and trusted, who enjoyed every moment, who knew that she could bring a child into this world through love. And now she was leaving; our precious girl was leaving us.

In the morning, brain stem tests were planned so that they could go through everything necessary in order to switch the machines off. As we waited for that horrible step, I whispered to Pete, 'Lock the door. Lock it and don't let them in and then it won't happen.'

'They have to come in, Mandy – it's just what has to happen.'

The tests went ahead and they warned us that there is something called a Lazarus Effect, which can happen in some patients after they've died. For some bizarre reason, the person sits up and looks as if they've come back to life before falling back down again. That's exactly what happened with Charlotte: she sat up and then just fell back onto the bed.

And that was that.

I held her hand and rubbed her face, but she was gone. Unable to tear ourselves away, we just told her how much we loved her over and over again. How would I cope without her? How would I face life without my little girl? Pete and I were due to be married the following week after all those years we'd had together and she was to be my maid-of-honour but now I would be planning her funeral.

I'd get on with it, I always did. But this? This was bigger than anything I could have imagined. The grief of losing Charlotte was way beyond the grief of losing my childhood because I knew that if I didn't have my kids, I wouldn't have survived – and this girl was the biggest part of that. I was never one to dwell on how hard life was, how bad things were for me, but this? This was something beyond comprehension, beyond any notion of fairness after all I'd been through, and I was in a complete daze.

We stayed for an hour or so, but what can you do? I had to leave my baby behind and go on with life. A white feather lay in the corridor as we walked out and I just hoped Charlotte had sent it.

I had so much to do with all the kids and getting things organised, with the funeral happening only a week later.

Rebecca and I sorted most of it out. Charlotte's order of service read:

A Celebration for the life of Charlotte Yousaf (Charl)
March 12th 1992 – August 13th 2011

We walked in to 'Love Story' by Taylor Swift before a
poem called 'Precious Sister' from all her siblings was read
out. I'll always remember the last lines:

I will look towards Heaven for I know I will see,
A star that will suddenly glow big and bright,
It will be my sister smiling …
And watching over me and my family.

Then the eulogy was read by the minister and there was a
reading of 'Letter from Heaven'. Charlotte was committed
and although I have given my heart in this book, I really
can't go there – I can't go back to that part of my life, to
the moment I saw the coffin leave. We all said 'The Lord's
Prayer' and then 'Stand by Me' by Usher was played.

There was another blessing and then we left to the
sound of Charlotte's favourite song, 'Saturday Night' by
Whigfield. She had always been so happy when that track
played and it was right that we should try and leave with
lovely thoughts of her, but my God, it was hard. I know we
have her eulogy somewhere, but I don't want to look for
it, neither does Pete nor any of the kids – no one wants to
go back there. I think this will resonate with a lot of people
who have grieved or are still grieving. I kept her room as it

was until we moved – now Charlotte's whole life is boxed up. I've kept everything – the last clothes she took off, the chewing gum that she left on her windowsill, every single thing, and I can't throw it away. When I first brought her ashes home, I wanted to buy a lovely new box to put them in but realised I couldn't as I wouldn't be able to throw the original container away. I have a tattoo of her name on my back and I thought I would get some of her ashes put into it, but I couldn't do that either as it would mean part of her would be separated.

It's all part and parcel of being a bereaved parent and nothing can prepare you for it because it should never happen. When Charlotte died, it was only natural that it changed me, but it made me determined to be as strong as I could possibly be, especially given that it was this incredible girl of mine who had given me such strength originally anyway. I could have gone weaker, but I chose the other route. Always tell your kids you love them – when they go to bed, when they walk out of the door, when you finish a phone call or message – always, always tell them you love them.

For a while afterwards, Pete wouldn't have any photos of Charlotte in the house, it hurt him too much. One day we were out shopping and I had a trolley full of things. The woman scanning it all said, 'Oh, you've got a lot there,' and Pete replied, 'Yeah, we've got a lot of children!'

'How many?' she asked.

'We had 11, but we've only got 10 now,' he replied.

I went mad, I was screaming and shouting in the supermarket.

'No! We've got 11!' I said over and over. 'We've got 11!'

I hated that he seemed to be denying her but that was his way of coping. I made sure all the photographs went back up after that.

I want Charlotte to know that we're getting through, that we're all still here. I'm glad she has her dog Toffee with her now, but losing that dog was hard too as I felt it was the last part of Charlotte. I want her to know that there's a gap that will never be filled. The jigsaw will never be complete again. She was the one who wanted me to do this book, she thought everyone should know, and now I've done it but she isn't here to see it.

She was my best friend and I didn't get her for long enough, but my God, what an impact she made while she was here – what a wonderful, wonderful gift she was to the world.

15

Me

Mum died in 2014 and I only found out through social media. I'd had no contact with her since the September I finally left. Some of my girls had been having a nose online and they'd found Dad's social media, where he had posted that his wife had died.

I'm glad she'd dead because I hate her. When I read those words, when I saw the proof that she'd known all along, I felt a chill that any mother could behave that way. How could she stand by, knowing what her husband was doing to her child? How *could* she do that? The only time we ever connected was when I was pregnant with Ben, when she was my best friend, and that was it, that was the sum total of her mothering of me.

I still believe that she gave birth to me so he could abuse me. However, I do think she was a victim too. He was a bully and he often made her life miserable, but she should have taken us out of it. She took him back from the moment he left prison, having stood by him while he was in there. I can hold both things at the same time, the recognition that she was his victim and that she was a horrific mother. I can never forgive her but I can see that she wasn't living the perfect life.

I'm just waiting on Dad dying now and I'm not ashamed to say that I'll dance on his grave. But I'm still terrified of him. Any time he appears on the street, any time I see him, it takes me back and I panic. I still have triggers – I can't have treacle in the house and I hate crumpets. Just little things but my father loved those and if I see them being eaten, it takes me back to him.

I call him Nonce now, we all do. He's not my father, he's not my dad – he's just Nonce. I also hate my own name. I hear it being said from his lips and I want to be sick – Pete calls me Mutts and I'm usually being shouted as a mum or grandmother, which suits me just fine!

I survived it, and I'm still surviving. The only victim in this is Ben. He had no choice – his entire life is the way it is because of Nonce. I still get the same feeling in my stomach that I've always had when he's around, the one I got in the police station when I gave my interview and saw him walking down the corridor; the one I have whenever he's nearby. Even if I'm in town and haven't seen him yet, I know when I will. It's like a sixth sense, it's primal. The hairs on my arms stand up, my tummy starts somersaulting. It's as if there's a voice whispering, *He's close. He can get you.* To this day, I'm still terrified he'll take Ben. Keith Meadows – I can't call him Dad anymore – presents himself on social media as a great guy, the one who always fooled everyone. He's back in the heart of The Salvation Army, doing good deeds, helping the community, and no one seems to care that he's a convicted sex offender, that he did those terrible things to his own child. I know that my fear of him taking Ben is completely wrong; what would he do with him? Why would he want to look after a grown man who needs 24/7 care? It doesn't stop that fear existing, though – he could take my boy just like he tried to do from the start.

I want this book to make other people strong if it can. What my father did to me was never my fault and if other survivors are reading this, I want them to know it was never their fault either. I wasted years of my life feeling guilty for his actions. Keeping it quiet is protecting abusers so speak out if you can. Go to the police every day if you have to. Do it when they're alive, do it when they're dead, but do it if you can.

There are so many changes that need to be made but in terms of children born from rape, we need to see them as innocent victims. They need support and they need to know that they aren't evil, they have nothing to be ashamed of. Also, I really want anyone who ever uses the word 'incest' to think twice: it's not a relationship, there is no consent involved, it should never be in any official document or paper, it should never be used to report on abuse cases. It's a word that needs to completely die.

I was approached in 2022 by a woman called Sammy Woodhouse, who is herself a victim of horrendous abuse but now an incredible campaigner for all survivors. Sammy told me that she was making a documentary about women who had children as a result of rape and she'd like me to be involved. There were other women who told their stories, women from around the world, and there were also people who had been conceived from rape. When I told Sammy what had happened to me, I also said that no one had ever told me it wasn't my fault.

She did.

It was such an emotional moment, even though I hate to cry. I don't like people being nice to me, I can't take it, but I sobbed at that. It gave me validation after years of blaming myself after having it drilled into me that it *was* my fault. Her kindness and her support at that moment broke through to me and I did finally accept that I was never culpable. He chose it, he decided what to do, and it was never, ever down to me – I have nothing to be ashamed of, I was just a child. That doesn't mean that I sail through life. I still dissociate and I still pack things away. Everyone needs to find what works for them. If you want to scream it from the rooftops, do it; if you want to box it all away, do it; if you want counselling, do it. When you're a victim of abuse, when you've been told what to do for years, you've been controlled and exploited. I won't continue by telling you there's only one path through this, but I will tell you that whatever you choose, it's valid.

My relationship with Calvin is hard but I'm still here for him. If he came back tomorrow, I would hope I would open my arms to him but it would be difficult, I can't deny that, as I just see his father when I look at him. However, just like me, he's not to blame. This is what I desperately want to get over to people. When you have a baby through rape, even though your feelings for that child might be different to those you have for your other kids who weren't conceived that way, that doesn't mean you don't love them. It doesn't mean you wouldn't do everything in your power to protect them. It just means that you know what they came from, you know the poison that made them, and you try hard, so very hard, to get past that with an undying commitment and promise to look after them, because it kills you – it kills you that you still think, after all these years, it was all your fault.

Ben is 38 now, he's a grown man. At one point he weighed nearly 20 stone but I've had him on a diet and he has lost some of it. He can talk a bit, but not the way you and I would. He can't walk far, he has special shoes. He doesn't really enjoy anything but we still try to find little things. It's a lot for me but I'll look after him until my last breath, but I'm so angry that my father did that to him.

There's no hope for Ben. He can't be made 'better', can he? I don't wish Ben hadn't been born but I do wish he hadn't been born as he is. All of my day is spent with him but he's my responsibility, and I know that my daughters will look after him when I go.

I blame myself, of course I do. If that hadn't happened to me, he wouldn't be like he is, would he? If I had done something, *anything*, he wouldn't be like he is so it's my responsibility to give him the best life I can.

Someone said to me when I was writing this book, 'You run on guilt, don't you?' And I do, I absolutely do. There's no time for me – if I'm not looking after the kids, I'm cleaning. I'm a mum, I love them, this is all I need. I don't go out for coffee with friends, I don't go for nights out, Pete and I don't go to the cinema, but that's fine – it's the hand I've been dealt. Ben panics if I'm not here, so it's better that I stay at home and let him know I'm around.

I would say I don't cry, but by God, I've cried doing this book. I'm emotionally shattered as I've never before sat down and looked at my life, but how can I dwell on it? How can I ever not be there for my son? I don't have time for emotions, I keep myself too busy because if I let it all come through, I might break. That's not me. I'm Strong Mandy. I'm Mandy Who Copes. I'm not weak and I see emotion as weak when it comes from me – crying isn't something I can allow myself to indulge in. I've never even cried about Charlotte until now.

But you know what? I'm blessed. I have Pete, my kids and my grandkids.

I have to believe that I was strong, that I got through it and I made the life I have today, even if it doesn't have my Charlotte in it. But I do get cross at myself – I do question why I didn't stop him, why I didn't push him away or tell someone earlier. I'm angry that when I did finally escape, I let him drag me back again, that I didn't have enough about me to stay away when I got out. I'm furious that I allowed him to do all of those things he did to me for years and for Ben to be paying the price of it all. I know that the coercive control I suffered was the hardest thing in the world to break and, on top of that, I had babies to protect. I'd spent so many years trying to keep my father away from my sisters and then there were two other little ones to shield. It was never-ending, it was a battle and I got no respite. So, why do I still hate myself so much for being the one it all happened to?

It's not easy surviving, but what else is there?

A few years ago, I got as much as I could from my files – there wasn't much and I've put bits of it in my story where they fit, but it's a tiny pile for a life that was shattered. The small pile I have is mostly letters from solicitors and a few medical professionals. As I've said before, I don't know if we even had Social Services involvement when I was a child. I certainly don't remember anyone ever speaking to me or being there when I was around, so I wouldn't know what to ask for even if there is anything.

The Calderdale Social Services Department did summarise what was going on when initial contact was made with them in 1994 and it was only recently that I saw the pages that had been written about me. It was such a shock to see it all there in black and white, my life laid bare:

The background circumstances to the Hospital Team's contact with Amanda Meadows is as follows:

Miss Meadows commenced attendance at the Child Development Unit, Halifax General Hospital, in July 1988 with her son, Ben Meadows. At that time concerns were focused on his motor development. Also, he had a congenital heart condition.

At that time, Amanda [was living with her] parents, Jennifer and Keith Meadows [in Halifax]. Mr Meadows was employed as a caretaker at Calderdale College and was living in accommodation provided by the Local Authority. The family situation seemed unsettled with Mrs Meadows suffering from a psychiatric illness and having regular periods of in-patient treatment.

Over the years, Mandy Meadows has made individuals, Social Services and the Police aware that her father had been sexually abusing her. These allegations were investigated by the Police and Social Services on two occasions. On these occasions, Mandy withdrew her complaint and denied the allegations.

In 1990, Mandy disclosed to Mrs Carol Jones, Hospital Social Worker, that she was having an incestuous relationship with her father and the last time her father expected her to allow him to sleep with her was three weeks ago. She also believed that her son, Ben, is the child of this incestuous relationship with her father. She was unsure if Keith Meadows was the father of her second child, Calvin Meadows.

Mr and Mrs Meadows attended the birth of Calvin and Mr Meadows always attended the antenatal appointments with his daughter, Mandy.

Mrs Jones, Social Worker, first had contact with Mandy Meadows in May 1988 when a termination of pregnancy was requested. The termination was carried out in June 1988 when Ben was only a few months old.

After two Child Protection Case Conferences were convened [in September and October 1990], it was agreed that the Police would press their investigations, which resulted in hair samples being taken from Keith Meadows, his daughter Mandy and her two children,

Ben and Calvin, as it was suspected that Keith Meadows may be the father of one or both of these children. Their hair samples were sent for DNA testing.

Initially Ben Meadows was made a Ward of Court by his grandparents, supported by their daughter, Mandy. In October 1990, the Local Authority was denied leave by the High Court to intervene in the Wardship Application. However, following a second Case Conference [...] Calvin Meadows was made a Ward of Court.

[The following month, both] children were consolidated under the same wardship Proceedings, and an urgent hearing was recommended under a High Court Judge. He felt that [...] Ben should remain in the care of Mr and Mrs Meadows and Calvin in the care of his mother, Mandy Meadows, in Leeds.

[Ten days later, it was instructed that] Ben Meadows should be placed in the Interim Care and Control of the Local Authority so that he could reside with Foster Parents.

On 20.12.1990, Calvin Meadows was admitted to Foster Care for the purpose of respite for his mother, Mandy Meadows.

(1) Threats made against her by the family;

(2) Preset accommodation was unsuitable;

(3) No Social Services support over the Christmas period.

Calvin was returned to Mandy on 3.1.1991.

On 25.3.91, Mr Meadows was arrested and charged.

On 26.3.1991, Mandy Meadows gave a full statement to Halifax Police.

Also on 26.3.1991, Mr Meadows had admitted that he would plead guilty to one charge of indecent assault and two charges of incest. He had accepted that he was the father of both Ben and Calvin Meadows. He was bailed on condition:

> *(a) Not to interfere with prosecution witnesses (Mandy);*
>
> *or*
>
> *(b) To see the two grandchildren. (sic)*

[...] the ongoing rehabilitation plan with Ben back to the care of his mother continued and Ben returned [to her] on 4.7.1991.

Shortly before Mr Meadows appeared in Court there was an indication, via the Probation Service, that he was going to deny any sexual activity with his daughter until she became 18, in the hope of reducing the sentence. Mrs Jones had information from a Hospital Psychiatrist's notes referring to Mrs Jennifer Meadows, in which she referred to her husband's sexual activity with Mandy when she was only 11 years of age. This information was passed to Dr XX, who was completing the report on Mr Meadows for court.

Mr Keith Meadows appeared at Leeds Crown Court on 10.9.1999 and was given a three-year prison sentence by Judge Saville. Mr Meadows admitted four charges of incest with his daughter between October 1982 and January 1990. He denied two charges of incest. [Judge Saville] was quoted as saying: 'Incest by a father with a daughter is always a serious matter because it inevitably involves a father taking advantage of the experience and innocence of the daughter. You used her for your own sexual desires and the result is that she may have suffered emotional and psychological damage quite incalculable.'

I read that over and over again: 'Mrs Jones had information from a Hospital Psychiatrist's notes referring to Mrs Jennifer Meadows, in which she referred to her husband's sexual *activity with Mandy when she was only 11 years of age. This information was passed to Dr XX, who was completing the report on Mr Meadows for court.'*

What I can't understand is if the authorities knew that he'd been abusing me since that age – in my mother's own words – then how did my father get away with saying he had 'only' abused me four times after I was 16 in 1982? In fact, by claiming the first time was October 1982, he was making himself out to be such a good guy (again!) that he'd waited until the very month I turned 16 to have this so-called 'relationship' with me.

There is both power and frustration in seeing your life laid out like that – power in the validation, frustration in the fact that they got so much wrong, that they never joined the dots, and that they called it 'an incestuous relationship' throughout. There is one phrase in there about me 'allowing' him to 'sleep' with me that is completely and utterly offensive in my eyes, but how can I ever get over the documented fact that Mum reported seeing him raping me and nothing was ever done? No one tried to get me out, no one questioned me. It was just something to be noted in *her* records and brought out years later in a typed-up file.

So, what am I left with? Who is the woman writing this book?

I'm a wife (we did finally get married!), a mother, a grandmother.

I'm not weak, I'm strong.

I'm not a victim, I'm a survivor.

I'm not worthless, I'm loved.

It takes a lot for me to say anything nice about myself and I hate people telling me nice things, but in my heart of hearts, I know that I've done a good job. Pete and I made it in the end and more than 30 years since we first laid eyes on each other, we can still take on the world. We've made a wonderful family, raised fantastic kids, we now have grandkids to add to the mix, and I'm never happier than when we're all together. Will I sleep easier when my father is dead? I'd be lying if I said I wouldn't, but I will hold my head up proudly no matter what he's doing.

Abuse survivors have steel in their blood but that doesn't stop them hurting. We pick up the pieces for others, we fill every minute so that our minds don't wander, we fight unfathomable battles every single day – and we keep going. What was done to us was never our fault. We never asked for it and we never agreed to it. We were groomed, threatened, beaten, undermined and often despised, but do you know what? We're the strongest army out there because we still love.

I waited so long for someone to save me; I dreamed of it often, played out scenes in my head where someone else would swoop in and save little Mandy. I had it in me all along.

And that, that is what makes me proud of myself even in the darkest of times.

I saved me.

Epilogue

Dear Mutts

You've finally found your voice. It's taken years and years, but you have it now and it's a truly wonderful thing to see you tell your story on your terms.

You're so hard on yourself and I wish you could see how incredible you are. You didn't have much to say when I first met you and I knew there was something not quite right even though you were very good at covering things up. I remember he was always with you, he was always on the scene, and you just told me he hated Asians and was checking to see if you were with me, but that didn't sit right, I knew it was more than that. When I asked you and you said he was abusing you, I knew you had to get away and I admit that I never understood why you wouldn't just leave. It was as if you had a bond with him, but how could you?

All of those times I tried to get you to see that you had to leave, all of those times you said you couldn't, I just wanted us to be together and I couldn't get my head round feeling that you were choosing him over me. You've finally accepted that you did nothing wrong, this was all down to him. You never got help, you never got support, you never got justice, but still you fought. We didn't have an easy path to walk to be together, but we got there – thankfully, because all I ever wanted was you.

You've battled for so long. There were years when you wouldn't go into town, wouldn't even go shopping without me by your side, but you're not like that now and I do think it all changed when we lost Charlotte. That showed both of us that tomorrow isn't guaranteed, you have to grab what you can when you can, because you can lose it at any moment. After losing our little girl, we both know how delicate life is. It's hard to this day but I think Charlotte dying has hurt you more than anything, even more than what he did to you – however, it's also made you even stronger, which I didn't think was possible.

We have a wonderful life and it's all because of the woman you are. You take a backseat and do everything for all of us, you are the glue that holds our family together and I know that I would be nothing without you. I couldn't be prouder of you, I couldn't adore you more. You've come through everything and not only are you still standing, you're an inspiration to us all. You're the kindest woman there could ever be and I love you more than anything. You don't want a great deal from life – just a visit to Graceland! – but I would give you the world if I could.

I've loved you from the moment I set eyes on you, Mutts, and I'll love you until the end. You have no idea what an extraordinary woman you are and I hope that now your story is going out into the world, you'll finally be able to see just how much you've achieved.

I'm lucky. I'm a lucky, lucky man.

With all my love forever, Pete x

Acknowledgements

There are a number of people I'd like to thank, people who have made it possible for me to be the person I am today, which has given me the chance to get my story out there.

My ghostwriter, Linda Watson-Brown. What can I say? You've been fantastic, absolutely brilliant, and I even forgive you for making me cry practically every time we spoke! I can't believe you took the time to do this for me and I'll always be grateful.

Malcolm Johnson, the solicitor who has fought so hard for Ben – thank you for all you have done.

Sammy Woodhouse, whose BBC documentary, *Out of the Shadows: Born from Rape* (2023), allowed me to see the magnitude of this issue and connect with others going through the same.

Emma Ailes, the BBC journalist and producer who

started the process of giving me my voice.

Ciara Lloyd and everyone at John Blake Publishing for their understanding and compassion.

My children for loving me as much as I love them and, of course, my husband Pete. I love you so much for just being you. I love you always and forever. I love you for everything.